THE
ALL-WEATHER
TRADER

THE
ALL-WEATHER TRADER

MR. SERENITY'S THOUGHTS ON
TRADING COME **RAIN** OR **SHINE**

TOM BASSO

CONTENTS

INTRODUCTION

EVERY SMALL ACTION YOU TAKE INVOLVES RISK. THINK about your most common everyday occurrences: the drive to work, crossing the street, and absent-minded multitasking. These may not seem unsafe, but they can have dangerous consequences.

Risk is everywhere. Whether it's your well-being, your financial state, or any other important part of life, you are experiencing risk. It's unavoidable and will find its way to you.

It's unavoidable; fear is natural. A lingering fear has enveloped the investing world. It has created roadblocks by way of instilling anxiety into those who wish to enter the seemingly high-risk, high-reward arena of money management.

Think about what has happened in the financial markets over the last five decades:

GRAPHIC 1—THE DOW JONES INDUSTRIAL AVERAGE OVER THE LAST FIVE DECADES ($DOWI)

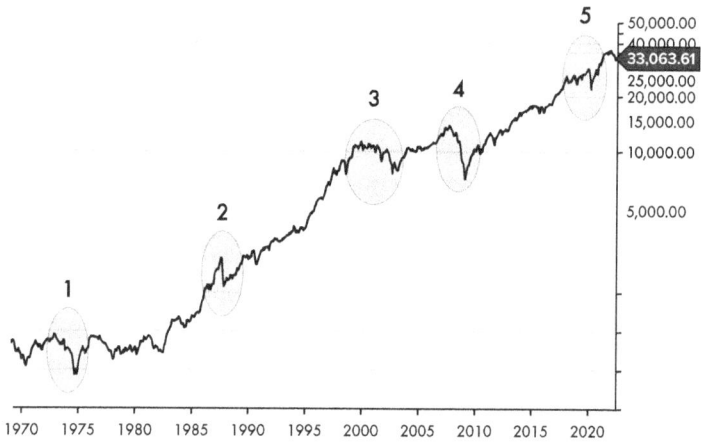

Source: Barchart.com.

The bear market of 1973–74, when the S&P 500 Index fell 45 percent.

1. Black Monday, October 19, 1987

2. The dot-com bubble burst in 2000

3. The housing crisis that led to an economic collapse from 2008 to 2009

4. The COVID-19 pandemic, which caused global economic chaos in 2020

These events resulted in disaster for families across the globe, causing some to lose all they had in a short amount of time. Some investors found themselves nearly out of the game. Witnessing these distressing events happen to friends and family has had an emotional effect on traders, and this has been going on for decades.

I have experienced this firsthand and am keenly aware of the risk that investors take when investing in any market. I saw this happen to my father in real time. As a letter carrier for the United States Postal Service, my father, Carlo Basso, had a good job. Having been born to Italian parents who suffered through the Great Depression, working at a steady job with a pension was about all he could have hoped for, which was a sentiment shared by a majority of his generation. They viewed the stock market like a casino—a *gamble* where every hand dealt could be the big payoff or a loss that could wipe away their entire stack of chips. Instead, faith was put into a steady paycheck, benefits, and a retirement plan.

Carlo Basso knew that he wanted more, and he wanted to invest. But he didn't want to be part of the *gamble*. He instead wanted to put his money somewhere more secure and less volatile. He took the money he had budgeted for savings and placed it into what he thought was the safest investment at the time: certificates of deposit with a local savings and loan. Investing in a savings and loan was the conservative route. He was not dealing in real estate or a volatile stock market. He had removed all his perceived risk and taken the safe path.

The savings and loan industry crashed shortly after this, in 1980, when short-term interest rates went higher than long-term rates and the yield curve inverted. After a $200 billion bailout from the government, these investors were made mostly whole and able to recoup much of their losses. Luckily, my father maintained his job with the Post Office so that he could continue to provide for his family and his three growing children.

GRAPHIC 2—A SUMMARY OF THE SAVINGS AND LOAN DEBACLE OF THE EARLY 1980s

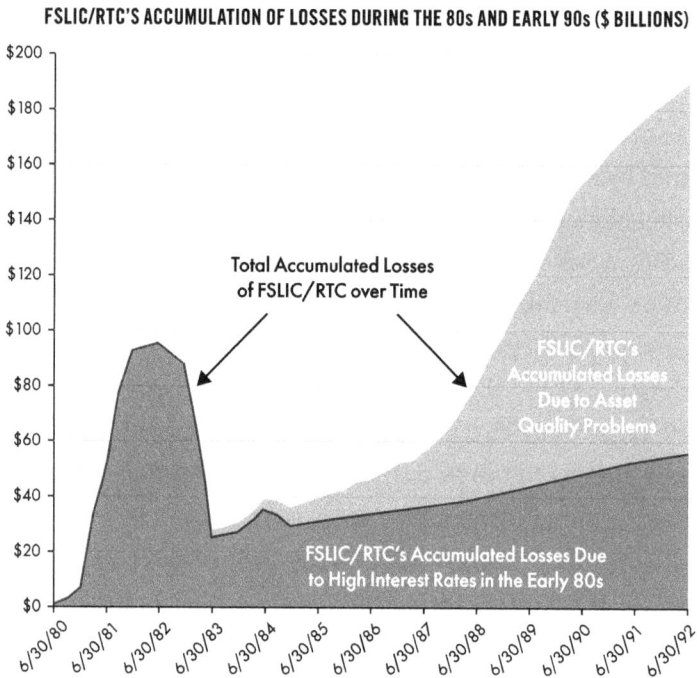

FSLIC/RTC'S ACCUMULATION OF LOSSES DURING THE 80s AND EARLY 90s ($ BILLIONS)

Total Accumulated Losses of FSLIC/RTC over Time

FSLIC/RTC's Accumulated Losses Due to Asset Quality Problems

FSLIC/RTC's Accumulated Losses Due to High Interest Rates in the Early 80s

Carlo's family was among the lucky few, but others weren't so fortunate during the savings and loan fallout. The same can be said for the Great Depression, Black Monday, the COVID pandemic, and any of the other famously dire movements in the stock market. Few were lucky or shrewd; most were not. The lesson I took from my father's run-in with the savings and loan crisis was that even when investing in the most seemingly risk-free environment, an investment is never truly risk-free. Things can change in an instant, and if your self-worth is wrapped up in one investment, and that investment is moving fast against you, you can find yourself with significant losses. I had not yet learned much about the power of diversification and attacking risk, which would ultimately become the core of my future career as a money manager.

In my years of managing other people's money, I've learned that no trader can hide from risk. It will find you. The only true way to prepare for risk isn't to hide from it, but to tackle it head-on. In this book I will describe a number of ways that I learned to attack risk and benefit from the process. All these ideas are simple enough that you can adopt the concepts, modify them to suit your own portfolio, or invent some new ways to improve your portfolio's performance and become an All-Weather Trader.

INVESTOR OR TRADER?

You may think of yourself as an investor because you are "in it for the long term." I have heard those exact words so many times. But here's a flash for everyone trying to manage your wealth: WE ARE ALL TRADERS! Buying anything with the intent to sell it somewhere down the road is trading. So, in this book I will use the title "trader" to label all of us tackling the challenge of dealing with financial markets.

CONSERVATIVE OR AGGRESSIVE?

You may think of yourself as one of two types of traders: conservative or aggressive. But I'd like to throw another curveball at you. Even though my dad thought of himself as "conservative," he wasn't in the end. He took on risk, and that risk was realized. So, from this point on in your trading journey, I want you to think of striving for better returns while reducing risks along the way. Where you end up doesn't have to be conservative or aggressive. It will be your own personalized way of dealing with your portfolio, no one else's.

LARGE OR SMALL PORTFOLIO?

You may have a smaller portfolio and are just starting out. Maybe you have only a few thousand dollars that you've scraped together to get started. I started out with a $2,000 margin account back in 1974, and I still remember it well. When I was a money manager at Trendstat Capital, my staff and I managed $600 million.

The ideas in this book may be easier to implement with massive amounts of money, but that doesn't mean that you can't apply the concepts provided to smaller amounts as well. I have created many examples in the book using nice large, round number portfolios like $100,000 or $1,000,000 or even $10,000,000 in order to make the explanations mathematically simple and easy to absorb. I know that most are not trading those sizes. I am simply trying to show the effect of the All-Weather concepts that I'm explaining. These concepts can be used by anyone, no matter the size of their portfolio.

Smaller portfolios will suffer from what I call granularity. In other words, the predictability of using the concept is not as perfectly predictive with a smaller portfolio as with a larger portfolio. The results are a bit more hit-or-miss statistically speaking. Just like looking at a granular picture on your TV with all sorts of black dots throughout the picture, granular results in trading mean that even though a trading concept works statistically on a large sample of trades, there's a chance that at any moment, it may not. The larger the sample size and the larger the portfolio, the less likelihood of granularity you'll have in applying the concepts.

It's like taking a poll. If I ask ten people a poll question and get an answer that six people feel one way and four feel the other, I have a little glimpse of what their mood is. However, if I take a poll of 10,000 people and ask the same question, I get a less granular answer to their mood. If 7,263 people answer the poll one way and 2,737 answer the other, I have a lot more confidence that result is a true representation of the mood of this larger sample size. Both sample sizes are what they are. The larger-sized sample is less granular and more accurate.

If you're starting small, take on the challenge of making your portfolio grow. Work a bit harder at your day job, save what you can, and add it to your trading account. Grow your portfolio by using sound All-Weather techniques. If you persist in doing these things, you may be managing millions one day in the future.

HE OR SHE?

I get statistics from my website, enjoytheride.world, that tell me that more than 80 percent of my followers and visitors to the site are males. I do get questions every now and then from you ladies out there, but trading seems to still be an overwhelmingly male endeavor, so to be efficient, I will use "he" when referring to a trader. Assume it is the person doing the trading, male, female, or any of the other genders that are out there these days.

THE LINGERING PROBLEM IN MONEY MANAGEMENT

The landscape of money management is much different today from prior decades. I've studied markets for half a century and recently have seen dramatic shifts in investor behavior. Technology has made it possible to see up-to-the-second quotes, which means that volatility can be measured by the minute. Traders experience these wild swings, good and bad. The panic that sets in for traders is real and happens quickly.

Trading is about mitigating risk. Why not *attack risk*, so that you can arrive at the battlefield on your own terms, rather than the market's? This is what I call being an All-Weather Trader.

All-Weather Trading

The major stock markets are volatile; yet this is where most retail investors want to put their money. The reason is simple. Stocks are easy to understand, and they capture all the media attention. Stocks are also deeply liquid in many cases, so billions of dollars can easily be moved from one stock to another. Many believe that the high risk of investing in the stock market produces the potential for high returns. A smooth equity curve up and to the right—that's what all my investment clients wanted to see during my Trendstat Capital years.

Losses, however, are nearly impossible to eliminate because it's not possible always to be on the correct side of a market. I don't believe that there is anyone out there who can predict what will occur on any given day or week. All the markets have an insidious way of fooling a majority of traders a majority of the time. However, thinking of risk and possible losses as an opportunity can put the trader into the proper frame of mind for an All-Weather approach to investing. Although attacking risk can help mitigate some of those bad days, there will still be a few that show up. It is part of this challenge we call trading.

The All-Weather Trader will attempt to hedge away much of the volatility seen in the markets, so it should be no surprise that I will mention volatility quite often. With all the major swings we are witnessing in areas like tech stock prices, companies going public, and cryptocurrencies, there is plenty of volatility to talk about. The All-Weather Trader uses that volatility to his benefit, rather than hiding from it. Just like a cowboy tries to tame the wild stallion to create a great working horse, the All-Weather Trader is focused on where the volatility might come from and how he can proactively use it to his advantage in making the account less volatile. He is not resorting to avoiding risk and thus suffering the lower returns that can accompany "conservative" investing.

The All-Weather Trader is not trying to eliminate stocks or any particular market. In fact, that trader is trying to capture returns wherever they might be found. This philosophy toward trading simply expands the investment universe and spreads assets across multiple avenues and continents in a strategic way, creating the ability to capture returns in any economic climate.

This is a philosophy toward trading that I have successfully implemented many times over. It isn't something that I came up with yesterday and put into play. I have been at this game for quite some time. It has been a process that has taken time to develop, adjust, and execute, but the concept has done nothing but perform well for me, providing steady, consistent results over time while allowing me a peaceful mindset.

THERE IS NO "EASY" BUTTON

As money managers, we are well aware of the mantra from our clients:

Make me a good return with minimal risk.

This universal investment objective seems to glue itself into the minds of many retail investors today. The reason is that the available technology makes it seem as though this is possible. In a world where social media displays people showcasing great returns and self-proclaimed experts boasting that they know which company will be the next Amazon, it's common for people to think these windfalls are possible.

However, in the real world of investing, I know that risk is everywhere. There are no guaranteed winners, and nobody can really determine which investments will be losers. There exists a risk and reward relationship, and to reap that reward, you must take that risk.

By creating an All-Weather Trading Plan, I believe you can go after those returns you seek, not worrying about what is going to happen next, and yes, sleep well at night like Mr. Serenity!

1

WHAT'S THE PERFECT INVESTMENT?

THE PERFECT INVESTMENT LOOKS SOMETHING LIKE this: a 20 percent return on your investments year over year; very little exposure to different markets (making it simple to track price movements); and an online platform that forecasts market fluctuations with 100 percent accuracy and zero risk.

So, where can someone go to find this magical formula? You know the answer: **NOWHERE!** This idea of having definitive answers to every challenge in the markets is a myth. It doesn't exist. If it did, money managers would be fighting and clawing their way into a position inside this perfect strategy. Everyone would already know where best to place their funds.

Certain investment strategies can seem like they are perfect. When one investor sees another doing well, they want in on the "secret" so they can improve their returns also. The idea of life-changing wealth is the lure that entices so many to search for the perfect investment. Whether they implement the strategy themselves or hire a money manager to do it for them, investors simply want the safety and security of knowing that their account is consistently and significantly increasing.

When returns drop? Well, that's when panic sets in. It can lead to friction between investors and their financial advisors. Investors have an underlying assumption that the financial advisor holds a single key that unlocks this magic formula that will turn things around. Yet this isn't possible because there is no universal strategy that is optimal for every client.

Traders will see drawdowns along the way. Panic can set in there as well, making decisions on what and when to buy or sell hard to execute. This angst can cause the trader to abandon a well-thought-out plan and seek new strategies that sound good at the time. Believe me, the grass is not greener on the other side in trading. There is no one universal way to getting it done.

As traders, we're all aware that there is no perfect strategy, yet we continue to seek it. Each of us, retail trader and money manager alike, is consistently adjusting and trying to find that single strategy we all know to be impossible to reach. Trading reminds me of golf. There is a perfect round (eighteen birdies) to strive for, but it has never happened.

Sticking to the golf analogy, financial advisors could be viewed as golf club pros. Club pros know everything about the course. They talk to golfers coming into the pro shop to answer questions on the upcoming round. They study the daily trends and know what's been going well and where people have been struggling. These are the reasons many golfers like to ask them for advice before heading out to the first tee.

Yet while they have this breadth of knowledge, they can't give the same pointers to every golfer who approaches them. Each golfer is different. Each has different skill sets. A scratch golfer and a high handicapper cannot be given the same tips for playing the course, nor would they desire such information. Each golfer also has his own version of a good score. For that high handicapper, shooting a ninety could be a great day. Yet, for the scratch golfer, a ninety could be a day they'd like to forget!

Golfers vary just as traders vary. Each trader comes to the challenge with a finite amount of assets to trade, a current skill set, a finite amount of time he can afford in developing a strategy, and a certain amount of time he can dedicate to the everyday execution of whatever strategy he develops. It would be crazy for any trader to attempt to do exactly what I do, the same way it would be crazy for me to attempt to copy Jack Nicklaus or Tiger Woods out on the golf course. Each of us has an individual financial puzzle to solve, and each trader will have a different solution to his personal puzzle. My goal here is to get you thinking about the philosophy of becoming an All-Weather

Trader and to help you develop you own personalized trading strategy—one that can weather the storms ahead while enjoying the good times.

THE GAME OF MONEY

Golf is a game that many of us have played. Whether you enjoy golfing or you don't, there is one fact that we can all find interesting: nobody has ever gotten a perfect score. For a traditional-sized golf course, a perfect score is somewhere around fifty-four, which means you would swing your club a total of fifty-four times from the opening tee until you sink the last putt on the eighteenth green.

It's incredible that there's never been a perfect score in a sport that dates back to the fifteenth century. Millions of players have come and gone. In recent decades especially, professional golfing has become a global interest. Parents now raise their children from a very young age to become golfers with aspirations of joining the PGA Tour and making a name for themselves. Tiger Woods, Phil Mickelson, and Annika Sorenstam are all household names with many wins under their belts, and yet none has been able to shoot a perfect score. When interviewed after a personal best round, they are always able to say, "Well if I had made that eight-footer on the seventh hole, I would have shot one better."

This isn't to say these golfers aren't great. The simple fact is that human error makes it impossible to shoot every shot perfectly. There are too many variables at play. In a game where so many swings are taken, it's inevitable that a ball will be sliced. Or hooked. Or you will misread a putt on a fast green, and you'll send your ball into the express lane, back down a hill and into the rough.

Whether you are a pro golfer or a money manager who enjoys hitting the links on occasion, the goal when you step out onto the course is to do one thing: be better than you were the previous outing. The goal is to try to eliminate the errors that you have experienced in your game and enjoy the ride while doing it.

When you are practicing, you are trying to get better. You practice until the weakest part of your game goes away and you find a *new* weakness to work on. There was a time in Tiger Woods's career when he drove the ball more than 315 yards off the tee. In his prime, his drive was something incredible to witness. But he still wasn't able to shoot a perfect score, so he was out there practicing with everybody else.

Trading is the same thing. Nobody has ever gotten a perfect score in investing, and there isn't a money manager in the world who would claim to have done so.

Trading, like golf, takes consistent practice. The trader can only try to do his best, continue practicing and working toward getting better at the process. In golf, the risk of slicing or hooking a shot remains constant with every swing you take. Risk is inevitable. As long as you are playing the course, you are taking risk.

The same thing can be said of investing; risk is all around you. The winning strategy here is to *mitigate* that risk. For example, if you had a strategy in place that could potentially gain you a 12 percent return yet contains a lot of risk, would it be better to have a 10 percent return instead if the risk were massively downsized? Would the two-percentage-point trade-off be worth it? Does it make sense mathematically? How about psychologically? Will you sleep better at night knowing there is less of a chance of risk coming in and interrupting your returns while you sleep?

In golf, that perfect score is impossible to shoot, but that shouldn't stop you from going out and practicing. You then put yourself in the best possible position to have a great outing. Trading brings the same mentality: you can continually try to lessen all risk and improve your chances of having a good outing with your portfolio. My advice to you is to accept the fact that you will never actually have the perfect, zero-risk portfolio or the perfect trading strategy. All you can do is continue to weigh options, study the data, adjust your strategies, and put yourself in the best possible position for success. After doing all that, as I've often said to my trader friends, you need to "Enjoy the Ride!"

NET WORTH VERSUS NET WEALTH

Future plans rely pretty heavily on what you are able to accomplish with your investments. It's why this idea of risk tends to instill fear into us, because when we take risks, we could be chancing some loss of a significant portion of our portfolio, and that muddies our vision of the future. Knowing you have a $10 million payment coming to you next year would allow you to plan for it. Knowing the timing would give you the schedule for your work, and by the time it arrived, you would hopefully be prepared to deal with it.

Not knowing what the future holds is more challenging. You don't know if your trading strategy will be profitable or not. You don't know how much you'll be able to add to your portfolio over time. You don't know what the market will do. Your entire financial plan is like a dense cloud you can't see through. How can that not be stressful to figure out?

So many focus on the universal investment objective: make a lot of money with little risk, increasing your net worth over time. I have a different mindset when it comes to the objective of the preservation of assets. What everyone should be truly looking to do is to preserve their *net wealth*, not their *net worth*. There's a difference between the two. *Net worth* is the blanket term everyone jumps to when it comes to placing a value on assets. It's the *net wealth*, however, that gives you purchasing power. *Net worth* is simply subtracting what you owe from what you own. Your *net wealth* is what you can buy with your net worth.

Within the investing world, this idea of preserving assets should take precedence over anything else. If you want a fresh perspective, try focusing on that net wealth concept. You can make all the returns you want on a given asset class, but if those returns are being outweighed by a negative monetary event, those gains will be in vain. Take, for instance, investment gains against the value of a given currency. If you are able to secure an 8 percent gain over a given period of time in a U.S.-based investment, but the U.S. dollar drops 9 percent in its purchasing power, have you really won in the end? Sure, the numeric value shows a gain in your net worth, but when you factor in the value of the dollar, the end result is a loss in net wealth and purchasing power.

Another example of this is in the savings or money market accounts many people use to store their cash. Currently, these accounts pay an annual yield of half a percent at most. When you take into consideration the fact that inflation has been right around 8 percent per year in recent months, as of this writing, one actually *loses* net wealth by investing in one of these accounts. As the cash sits, it loses purchasing power.

Every currency in the world has consistently inflated. The U.S. dollar as well as many other foreign currencies have been deteriorating at a pace so rapid that it's almost as if they are at a race to the bottom, and all the countries are trying really hard to win the race. Crazy times!

Of course, things can change rapidly. At the time I am writing this book, various currencies are all in a tailspin and cryptocurrencies are sitting in the spotlight. Will this trend continue in the years and decades to come? It's quite possible. However, don't forget to take regulations and restrictions into play. Remember that nations will create laws to govern in their best interests, and you will need to closely monitor these if you want to preserve your net wealth.

THERE'S NO PIE IN THE SKY

Rules, regulations, outside factors, and myths aside, the perfect investment still couldn't exist. There are too many forces that interfere with the process. There is too much information for us to see that influences the decisions we will make. Journals, newspapers, business channels, podcasts, or even conversations with your colleagues or neighbors could pull you into a new way of thinking. It's why buy-and-hold strategies never seem to work. There is too much persuasion all around us clouding our thinking and causing us to move on to the next investment.

How many times have you caught wind of a trending asset from a friend? How many texts have you received telling you to look into a newly listed cryptocurrency, an upcoming initial public offering (IPO), or some other promising trend? What have these conversations done to the comfort level with your current strategy? If you're like 99 percent of the trading world, news of this sort stimulates you to consider abandoning your well-laid-out strategy and move on to something else.

The subject of money and investments comes up all the time in your everyday life. It's impossible for anyone to put funds into an investment and then not look at it again for twenty years. That's true for both money managers *and* their clients. Becoming an All-Weather Trader takes this factor into consideration and helps to eliminate that desire to be always invested in all the correct markets.

My mentality, which I will discuss thoroughly in Chapter 11, plays a significant role in how I manage my investments to keep distractions to a minimum. I've been trading, either for clients or for myself, for about fifty years now, and I have seen plenty of traders fall into the emotional trap of chasing hot strategies and returns. That's why the approach I share with you inside this book has been designed with this in mind. It's an investment philosophy that not only diversifies against loss, but against your emotional desire to make drastic changes based on the information you hear every day that can distract you from your well-thought-out plan.

DRAWDOWNS AND RECOVERIES ARE NOT SYMMETRICAL!

This has been covered in many places in the financial press, but it bears repeating here. Every time you have a drawdown, it requires you to make more percent return than the depth of the drawdown, just to get back to breakeven, where you started the drawdown. Examine the math in the table below:

GRAPHIC 3—DRAWDOWN AND REQUIRED RECOVERY PERCENTAGES

DEPTH OF DRAWDOWN %	REQUIRED RECOVERY % TO BREAK EVEN
-1.00	+1.01
-5.00	+5.26
-10.00	+11.11
-20.00	+25.00
-30.00	+42.86
-40.00	+66.67
-50.00	100.00

If a trader can keep the drawdown smallish, say less than 20 percent, it isn't an unsurmountable challenge to make enough profit to get back to new highs on the equity curve. But let the drawdowns get away from you to uncomfortable levels, and you now face a greater challenge requiring some fairly sizeable returns to recovery to breakeven and beyond.

BE PREPARED

There is no downside to being prepared. Humans prepare for storms by stocking up on water, paper products, and canned goods. We prepare ourselves to go weeks on end without food and water in an age when technology can have drones fly products to us. If we are willing to overprepare for things that have to do with our health and survival, we should have no issues preparing for events pertaining to our financial well-being.

There is no perfect investment, but there are still key metrics to put in place that can get you as close to perfect as is reasonable. For starters, know what you can tolerate when it comes to risk.

For my father, risk-taking wasn't a part of his strategy. He desired to have a safe investment that would grow slowly over time. Compare that to many of the tech stock investors of today and you can get a glimpse of people on two opposite ends of the risk spectrum. If you don't calculate risk before you invest, your assets could end up on a small ship in large waves.

The next step is to identify the potential risks. Are you looking at historical trends, asking questions, and reading books like this one to broaden your knowledge? Are you looking at liquidity and costs and running any simulations of any particular strategy you are considering? By doing these things, you are better prepared to deal with so many more scenarios than the average person.

I wasn't born knowing all the secrets. I had to first learn to manage my own assets as a young man. I then spent twenty-eight years in the money management industry as both an SEC-registered investment advisor and CFTC-registered commodities trader. I also had a two-decade run in currency trading. I then went into retirement in 2003 and spent almost two decades designing and running trading strategies for our own portfolios. I have been at this for decades, working on separate strategies designed to attack one form of risk or another. This book is the culmination of a lifetime of learning, adjusting, and having it come together in a mentality that I truly believe anyone can adapt to his own situation. It is a culmination of all the things that I've learned. I have dealt with risk for a half a century, exposing it, attacking it, and managing it. Risk has certainly dealt me some blows in the past, but the time and energy I spend in dealing with risk is what has allowed me to come out on the other side of the storm. Preparation is what enabled me to have the confidence to write this book and to affect the lives of others looking to take that risk head-on.

There may not be a perfect investment or strategy, but there is a perfect philosophical approach to the challenge, and that's to continually study and to be prepared for what's to come. Just like the weather, it's always changing, and it's handy to have an umbrella around, just in case.

2

CREATING MY ALL-WEATHER PHILOSOPHY

INVESTORS AND MONEY MANAGERS ALIKE KNOW THERE is no perfect investment. The contents of the previous chapter are not new to anyone who has had even the slightest bit of exposure to the markets. Volatility is to be expected, as is loss. Yet we are continually infatuated by the success of others who perform better than we do. The goal we've been sold is to win the current battle rather than focusing on winning the war.

Firms and investors implement different strategies on all levels, and the underlying concept of each is to deal with risk. Which is the best-performing market? Where has the money been flowing, and where have been the largest returns? It's this short-term mindset that lands many investors in a short-term investment concept that many times does not remain in the portfolio very long. Once again, these traders look to win the battle and forget about winning the war. They get mired in a continual stream of what they think are sensible decisions that don't seem to work out the way they would have hoped, and then they move on to the next great idea. Move, get disappointed, and repeat. Not an enjoyable ride at all.

I have seen the writing on the wall for many years now. Traders rarely see a complete trading strategy that covers all aspects of being an All-Weather Trader. When markets swing heavily in one direction, one part of the trader's thinking will be to bail out of this thing that is going against him. Another part of the brain is thinking, "This thing is cheap now. Perhaps I should buy some more of it." Then movement back the other way brings the numbers back to normal, and thoughts change once again. This idea that you are always fighting with yourself and any advisors you are listening to causes a lot of stress and doubt and ends up being a terrible way to trade, since the trader really doesn't have a strategy. Many are making it up on the fly as the markets throw a variety of conditions and movements at them.

TEST YOURSELF FOR BIASES

Becoming an All-Weather Trader solves several problems in one shot. It not only provides ways of participating in positive moves for the portfolio with a reduced likelihood of a complete breakdown, enabling the trader to sleep peacefully at night, but it also simplifies the goals of the trading process. It directly attempts to deal with various forms of risk that the trader knows exist. It attacks those risks directly, which can give the trader some sense of control. Consciously, traders will bring all their biases to the party. Subconsciously, traders prefer an All-Weather approach. I know because of a simple test that you yourself can take.

Let's create a table of various return streams blended at various levels and let you pick what you might prefer. I'm not telling you the details, but these are actual historical returns in widely available indices at various allocation levels. At this point, study the data and decide for yourself which strategy you believe would be the best for you. Ask yourself why it would be optimal, perhaps even writing down the reasons. These annual return statistics are actual results over a twenty-one-year period of history. Which strategy is your personal winner?

GRAPHIC 4—WHICH INVESTMENT TASTES THE BEST TO YOU?

YEAR	A	B	C	D	E
0	-9.1%	11.6%	11.7%	1.3%	1.3%
1	-11.9%	8.4%	-0.1%	-1.7%	-6.0%
2	-22.1%	10.3%	26.1%	-5.9%	2.0%
3	28.7%	4.1%	11.9%	16.4%	20.3%
4	10.9%	4.3%	2.7%	7.6%	6.8%
5	4.9%	2.4%	0.7%	3.7%	2.8%
6	15.8%	4.3%	8.2%	10.1%	12.0%
7	5.5%	7.0%	8.6%	6.2%	7.0%
8	-37.0%	5.2%	20.9%	-15.9%	-8.1%
9	26.5%	5.9%	-4.8%	16.2%	10.8%
10	15.1%	6.5%	13.1%	10.8%	14.1%
11	2.1%	7.8%	-7.9%	5.0%	-2.9%
12	16.0%	4.2%	-3.5%	10.1%	6.2%
13	32.4%	-2.0%	2.7%	15.2%	17.5%
14	13.7%	6.0%	19.7%	9.8%	16.7%
15	1.4%	0.5%	0.0%	1.0%	0.7%
16	12.0%	2.6%	-6.1%	7.3%	2.9%
17	21.8%	3.5%	2.2%	12.7%	12.0%
18	-4.4%	0.0%	-8.1%	-2.2%	-6.2%
19	31.5%	8.7%	9.2%	20.1%	20.4%
20	18.8%	7.4%	6.3%	13.1%	12.5%
Annualized Return	6.6%	5.1%	5.0%	6.4%	6.5%
Worst Year	-37.0%	-2.0%	-8.1%	-15.9%	-8.1%

Now see what you selected.

GRAPHIC 5—INVESTMENT CHOICES WITH LABELS

YEAR	STOCKS S&P 500 TR	BONDS BARCLAY US AGG TR	MANAGED FUTURES SG TREND	50/50 STOCKS/ BONDS	50/50 STOCKS/ FUTURES
0	-9.1%	11.6%	11.7%	1.3%	1.3%
1	-11.9%	8.4%	-0.1%	-1.7%	-6.0%
2	-22.1%	10.3%	26.1%	-5.9%	2.0%
3	28.7%	4.1%	11.9%	16.4%	20.3%
4	10.9%	4.3%	2.7%	7.6%	6.8%
5	4.9%	2.4%	0.7%	3.7%	2.8%
6	15.8%	4.3%	8.2%	10.1%	12.0%
7	5.5%	7.0%	8.6%	6.2%	7.0%
8	-37.0%	5.2%	20.9%	-15.9%	-8.1%
9	26.5%	5.9%	-4.8%	16.2%	10.8%
10	15.1%	6.5%	13.1%	10.8%	14.1%
11	2.1%	7.8%	-7.9%	5.0%	-2.9%
12	16.0%	4.2%	-3.5%	10.1%	6.2%
13	32.4%	-2.0%	2.7%	15.2%	17.5%
14	13.7%	6.0%	19.7%	9.8%	16.7%
15	1.4%	0.5%	0.0%	1.0%	0.7%
16	12.0%	2.6%	-6.1%	7.3%	2.9%
17	21.8%	3.5%	2.2%	12.7%	12.0%
18	-4.4%	0.0%	-8.1%	-2.2%	-6.2%
19	31.5%	8.7%	9.2%	20.1%	20.4%
20	18.8%	7.4%	6.3%	13.1%	12.5%
Annualized Return	6.6%	5.1%	5.0%	6.4%	6.5%
Worst Year	-37.0%	-2.0%	-8.1%	-15.9%	-8.1%

I'm guessing you selected Choice E, which is the mix of 50 percent managed futures and 50 percent stocks. Why? These five strategies had returns in the same ballpark (between +5.0 to +6.6 percent), while the worst years were dramatically different (-2.0 to -37.0 percent). And why would I assume you didn't choose stocks or managed futures by themselves? That's simple: fewer returns with same or worse risk numbers.

This simple example shows some interesting truths. Given the labels ahead of time with no data, would you have picked a 50/50 mix of futures and stocks? Be honest with yourself. You might think futures too risky or say, "I don't know anything about that area of investing." It would be discarded for various reasons.

However, when forced to be impartial, people tend to make logical decisions. Where a person with biases might choose to invest in growth stocks, they wouldn't do the same when going into a similar scenario with only the data available. The lesson to be learned here is: let's get rid of the labels, the biases, the images of various investments, and take on the mental challenge of figuring out the best approach to trading for each of our personal financial puzzles. Why limit our tools? Let's keep as many alternatives open to solving this puzzle as we can.

STRATEGY IS IMPORTANT, NOT LABELS

I remember an interesting Saturday morning outside of St. Louis. I was invited to speak to a group of retail investors about a very low-leveraged futures trading program. It was basically going to trade in about twenty markets at face value. Zero leverage, zero chance of a margin call, zero problems with compliance, and extremely boring returns. I started the presentation off with an exercise in labeling various investments from conservative to risky based on solely the name of the investment. I asked the group to number them from 1 to 8, 1 being the riskiest and 8 being the least risky. I asked the group if they had any questions, and there being none, I had them take the survey. Seemed simple enough. Everyone was done quickly. You may want to rank them yourself, just for fun.

GRAPHIC 6—RISK RANKING VARIOUS INVESTMENTS— (1–8, 8 BEING RISKIEST)

INVESTMENT	RANK
Treasury Bonds	
Futures	
Commodities	
Stocks	
Mutual Funds	
FOREX Currencies	
Real Estate	
Gold	

I then asked the group to pass their papers in, and we totaled up the rankings. The results were not surprising to me.

GRAPHIC 7—RISK RANKING VARIOUS INVESTMENTS—RESULTS

INVESTMENT		RANK
	Treasury Bonds	8
	Futures	2
	Commodities	1
	Stocks	5
	Mutual Funds	6
	FOREX Currencies	3
	Real Estate	7
	Gold	4

This was a great lead-in for what I was about to discuss on stage. With this information, I then asked, "Does anybody want to know how I was going to manage risk in all these investments?" The entire room looked at me with blank stares. They had no idea what I was talking about, so I showed them the next page with a quick explanation of how I was thinking about managing the investments.

GRAPHIC 8—RISK RANKING VARIOUS INVESTMENTS— WITH STRATEGY DESCRIBED

INVESTMENT	RANK	MANAGEMENT STRATEGY
Treasury Bonds	8	10% margin cash trades, 30-year maturity (dangerous)
Futures	2	Trade at face value, no leverage, trend-following (boring)
Commo-dities	1	Trade at face value, no leverage, trend-following (watching paint dry)
Stocks	5	Buy initial public offerings and sell within 1 month (dicey)
Mutual Funds	6	Buy and hold a basket of funds (50% down risk in bear market)
FOREX Currencies	3	Trade on 3% margin, trend-following medium term (crazy)
Real Estate	7	No-money-down rentals (destined to blow up)
Gold	4	Collector coins (bid/ask spreads you could drive a truck through)

The light bulbs started to turn on. It now started to dawn on these "normal" investors that their image of various investment areas was biased based on what they had experienced, heard from others, or simply on how the press treats that type of investment. The lesson everyone learned that day is that risk is highly dependent on *how* you are going to manage risk. If I wanted to spend some time on that list, I could either make every item conservative and boring or I could manage the investment in a way that would place the portfolio in harm's way. I could also dial it in somewhere between the two extremes. The important lesson is, "They should have asked me how I was going to manage those investments and gotten a sense of how much risk would be remaining depending on the strategies used."

It comes down to winning the war versus winning the battle. Marketing types may promote this idea of rapid growth potential through things like tech stocks, and when we see those who have won "big," we want to be a part of it. But that short, successful run is only a fraction of the overall picture, which is the war. Those who have their short-term wins may get all the attention at a moment in time, but it's the trader who is okay with forgoing the short-term instant gratification to win the war who will be the true long-term investing warrior.

This is the long-term philosophy that I have used in managing Trendstat's and my own portfolios. It has been tested by crashes in the stock market, short-term interest rates, crude oil price going negative, and many violent market movements caused by news, wars, pandemics, Federal Reserve actions, and economy-affecting weather. And, through it all, I just keep doing what

I do each day, peaceful in the knowledge that I have a complete trading strategy that addresses risk in up, down, and sideways market actions.

MY STORY

The very first encounter with this idea of portfolio protection came when I was a young, avid investor. As a paperboy, I bought a growth stock mutual fund at twelve years old with some of my savings, adding to it each month with my profits from delivering newspapers. With market swings during the '60s, it took until I was twenty-two years old coming out of Clarkson University as a chemical engineer to break even on that investment. I was *now* aware of risk.

My dad's savings and loan scenario had a great impact on me, and I wanted to ensure that I had proper investing strategies in place for myself as an adult. So although I was coming out of college with a chemical engineering degree, investing had always been something of great interest for me.

During my first job as a chemical engineer, I would have lunch with some fellow engineers—mostly chemical, but a few mechanical engineers were allowed into the mix at the table. We would discuss investing, mainly in the form of talking to a stockbroker. We were curious as to what we could do to enhance our portfolios. Most of my colleagues sought the advice of financial advisors or newsletters to help them with this struggle, and they had all heard the same things: *you need to buy and hold stocks for the long-term, and timing the market doesn't work.*

It seemed to me as if every professional in the investing world was appeasing people with this idea of *be patient with the long-term stock strategy, and it will work*. But people aren't built that way. They can't sit back and watch as their net wealth fluctuates wildly. A 20 percent loss cannot simply be ignored. The idea of taking this approach might sound good on paper, but an investor would rarely allow this to go on without at least having some comment or suggestion about alternative investments that they should consider.

Listening to many of these conversations with my colleagues and researching strategies myself, I came to realize that there had to be a better solution. There was simply no way that every investor was accepting their stock market losses as the status quo. More importantly, there was no way those who invested through a money manager weren't picking up the phone at least once a week to call and question the methods at hand.

That's when I started looking into futures trading. The idea behind this was to offset the losses in stocks that would inevitably take place during a bear market. Doing so would allow my portfolio to be okay regardless of the volatility of the stock market. It wouldn't matter how bad losses were on a given day, week, month, or year because I was creating the potential for positive returns in other markets with diversified, non-correlated opportunities to profit. It took four years of futures trading before I had my first profitable year, a grueling learning curve. I considered it my four-year degree in the university of trading.

A few years later, I left my position as a chemical engineer and entered a professional career as a money manager. Yet as a money manager working with other people's money, I wasn't able to be as experimental as I was with my own cash. I needed to be more grounded and stick with an approach more aligned with expectations. We had to have strategies we could "sell" to the advisors and clients. Those expectations usually consisted of wanting to have our firm manage their pension's "stock portfolio." But when stock market losses resulted in client losses and the phone calls and redemptions started coming in, I quickly realized that something needed to change. I told my partners, "We need to do something, or we're not going to have a business if there's a major downturn."

I started to learn more, and it was during this time that my thinking crystallized. I realized there are a lot of different avenues you can take to try to mitigate risk, but people weren't taking them. Investment professionals were almost misleading their clients about the possibilities that using certain strategies could improve return-to-risk.

I took everything I learned during this time and used it to open Trendstat Capital. Our mission was to create strategies built around this concept of broad diversification, using stocks, futures, options, and mutual fund timing all at once, in a complete strategy that allowed for enhanced protection against risk.

The approach worked well. Diversifying into asset classes and strategies that were not correlated turned out to be something that saved a lot of potential loss. Yet there was still this lingering issue that was a result of how we humans think. We aren't wired to see loss and accept it. Although other areas of a portfolio were doing well and offsetting losses, the reports were still coming back to the individual with lots of detail due to rules and regulations in place at the time.

So, for example, if long stocks had a bad day and dropped 7 percent and we had futures positions that *increased by a similar amount*, the risk was averted. But individuals were getting separate reports, one for the long stocks and one for futures. While the futures report looked good, the long stocks report did not. This led to confusion. *"Why can't we skip the long stock position and put all of that into futures strategy? Then we'd be way ahead."* It was this sort of human nature that made me realize that clients are still going to be uncomfortable, and we needed to do more.

As the years went on, progress continued, and we did finally convince some clients to have stocks and futures in their portfolio. When Black Monday hit on October 19, 1987, the reports that had to go out to clients reinforced this idea that the separation was an issue. The Dow Jones plunged 22.6 percent that day, and although we had built portfolios with our clients that had offsetting positions in stocks and futures, those reports led to very strange reactions. The best example of this has me scratching my head to this day.

There was one large pension plan that we managed that had made a fraction of a percent on Black Monday, outperforming the Dow Jones Industrials by some 23 percent. I went into a normal quarterly meeting thinking we were heroes. We actually made a small profit when most stock portfolios had decreased by 20 percent or so. The board pointed out to me that they had made a huge overnight profit on the futures side of the portfolio and lost almost an equal amount on the stocks. These board members were Ph.D. physicists and knew their math.

They asked if they could have the winning side of the strategies and not the losing side. They requested removing long stocks from our strategy altogether. The "buy long only" stock portfolio was always bound to have its down moments, and the clients could not psychologically stand the heat. So, even though the equity value of their total account was up a very small amount for Black Monday, while most other pensions got killed that day, they fired us for the stock side of the portfolio and tried to keep us managing the futures hedge side of the portfolio. We fired them shortly after for not allowing us to do what was best for them as clients. We were not willing to trade the futures hedges without something to hedge against. It was very frustrating, but situations like that are just another reason I'm delighted to be retired from the business and not dealing with the strange ideas that clients come up with!

New strategies were developed, and we were having our successes at Trendstat. Diversifying into various asset classes that had a negative correlation to one another, we offset much of the risks that occurred in the time that followed. We did well enough to catch some attention from the industry.

I was featured in Jack Schwager's 1994 book, *The New Market Wizards*, where he named me "Mr. Serenity" because of my calm demeanor and unique, extremely diversified approach. Over the years, he had interviewed nothing but Wall Street traders who were high-strung and fast-paced. Yet I was serene compared to these other traders because I wasn't at the mercy of stock market risk or highly leveraged. I had strategies in place to reduce risk no matter what happened. I didn't have a name for it at the time, but it was basically an approach that allowed me to deal with a wide variety of conditions whatever market condition came my way. If only I could have thought of a good name for it...

3

MY DEVELOPMENT AS AN ALL-WEATHER TRADER

MY PURPOSE WITH THE LAST CHAPTER IS TO GIVE YOU an overview of the progression of my life, so that you can travel along with me through time and understand how one discovery led to another—and another and another. I feel like I'm still traveling down that path. In subsequent chapters, I am going to get into the details about these concepts. I'm hoping that you will be able to select your favorite ideas from the list and put them to work for yourself.

The very first thing that happened to me in my investing life was buying the mutual fund mentioned earlier. Little did I know that would take about twelve years to get back to even due to market fluctuations and extremely high management and sales fees.

I graduated from Clarkson University with a nice chemical engineer's salary, and I wanted to add some new investments to my portfolio. As I searched for better options for the future, I was looking for a way to prevent that twelve-year recovery from happening again. Or, at a minimum, I wanted to reduce the severity of the negative performing period. And I found a way.

We had a stock purchase program at my company, and I decided that if I set up a chart to give me up and down directions, I could buy stock on the upswings and sell it to avoid some of the risk of the downswings and use the company's money to finance the trades. This worked well with numerous moves becoming nicely profitable. Timing investments became one strategy I learned to use many ways to get closer to becoming an All-Weather Trader. More on that in Chapter 4.

A few years later, and four years after I started trading futures, I was finally achieving *breakeven results* in my portfolio. I was adding money into my futures portfolio and with some nice positive moves was rapidly increasing the size of equity in the account. I noticed that the profitable periods in futures had almost nothing whatsoever to do with when I was making profits in my stock portfolio. This meant true diversification and an additional layer of protection. When one market makes a profit while another loses, you have a more stable total result. Chapter 7 of this book is dedicated to extreme diversification and how to create it for your own portfolio.

Then I started my personal IRA. Inside the IRA is this magical world of deferred taxes. You can buy and sell, and realized gains and losses are treated the same as unrealized gains and losses. You don't pay any taxes until you remove assets from the IRA. I used what I learned from my company stock timing program and set up indicators to "time" various mutual funds. This was the start of what Trendstat used to do for clients in our mutual fund timing and sector timing programs. It was quite successful and a great way for smaller-sized clients to potentially pick up some of the upside potential of stocks and bonds without taking on all the risk with a buy and hold strategy in those same markets.

Back in my earlier years, exchange traded funds (ETFs) had not yet been invented, and I had to put up with calling in my trades on mutual funds at the end of every trading day. When my indicators flashed in a new up direction, I bought a stock mutual fund. When they gave me a down direction, I sold the stock fund and bought a money market mutual fund, earning the very nice interest available back in the '80s. Attacking the risk of a down stock market with timing became a very useful tool on my journey to becoming an All-Weather Trader. There's more detail in Chapter 4.

Since Trendstat Capital managed stock portfolios for some clients, and those clients didn't want to be trading those stocks in and out all the time, I developed the concept of dynamic hedging. I used a trend-following indicator to measure whether the stock market was moving up or down. When moving up, I didn't want to be hedged, so I let the portfolio's stock positions move with the wind at their back. But when the direction turned down, I simply put on a hedge to protect the current portfolio. Initially, I used short sales in an index exchange traded fund or bought one of the triple-leveraged, inverse ETFs, but today I prefer an index futures contract for various reasons. More on hedging later in Chapter 6.

Next in my development as an All-Weather Trader came the addition of various time frames. I noticed that during sideways periods in the markets, stocks generally bounced up and down rather quickly, never moving long enough in one direction to allow my longer-term trend-following models to produce a reasonable profit. The research showed me that with shorter-term time frames, I would have to trade far more frequently, and that was an issue when I first started down this All-Weather path. However, being an engineer by degree and eventually hiring great programmers, we realized that if we automated the process, we could handle the extra trades fairly easily.

I decided to create the shorter-term models and realized that because of the sensitivity of these new models, I could extract small profits over shorter periods of time. That created some time period diversification, since when markets were trending well, the longer-term models would keep me in and allow the profits to accumulate. However, when the markets spent more time in sideways action, the shorter-term models could produce some small profits to help the overall portfolio. I'll cover this in more detail in Chapter 8 on some things that you can do in sideways markets.

Next up I created a strategy that truly needed a sideways action to produce a profit. I decided to sell option credit spreads with a limited loss potential and a limited gain potential that were only seven days from expiring. That produced a return stream that was highly profitable if the market stayed right where it was or moved very little. This strategy was destined to lose money during robust market moves, but I already had that covered with my longer-term trend-following strategies. More details on option spreads and where and how I use them in Chapter 8.

Finally, I have watched with interest the development of crypto markets. There are literally thousands of cryptos out there trading on various platforms. Wanting to keep things simple, I created a shorter-term trend-following strategy to measure the directions of the crypto markets I was following. Since I know futures very well, I use the futures on Bitcoin and Ethereum cryptos as my trading vehicle. It's simple to obtain data, they're easy to trade, and I can easily put on positions in both up and down directions. That is one more unrelated return stream for my portfolios, and it has been very profitable over the last couple of years.

STILL IN DEVELOPMENT MODE

This chapter so far has covered years of development as an All-Weather Trader, but I don't feel that I'm as All-Weather as I would like to be. Just like the golfer who cannot shoot a "perfect score," I still see the potential to study my portfolio's weak spots and add new strategies to combat down periods in performance. I'm not sure that I will ever arrive at a final composition of strategies that will be "perfect," but I'm enjoying the ride trying to get there.

WHAT IS A COMPLETE TRADING STRATEGY?

I'VE OFTEN USED THE FOLLOWING FLOWCHART TO SHOW that a complete trading strategy is not just figuring out where to buy or sell. Most traders starting out in the trading business concentrate *only* on that, and it is a big mistake. Look at the flowchart and see how many of these boxes you've included in your process.

LET'S ADDRESS THE PARTS OF A COMPLETE TRADING STRATEGY ONE BY ONE

Belief: This is an important place to begin. As the late, great Dr. Van K. Tharp used to say, "You don't trade the markets. You trade your beliefs." You must come up with a belief that drives the potential profits in your strategy.

GRAPHIC 9—A COMPLETE TRADING STRATEGY

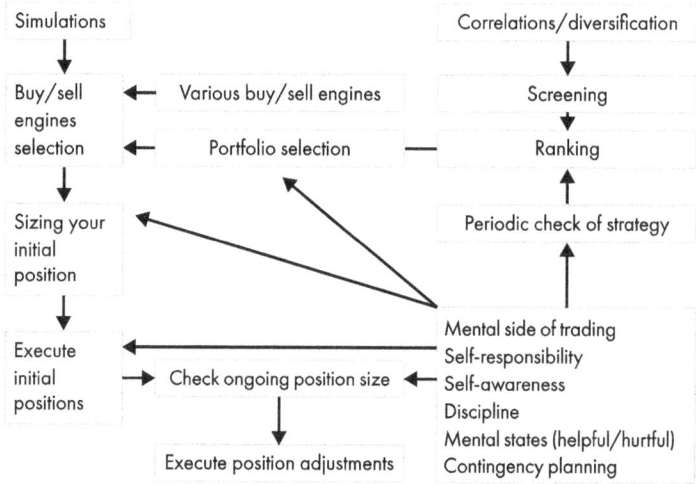

Objective: This should be the most important thing you put in place before even trying to design any strategy. It is the philosophy behind the strategy and guides you in the logic of what you are going to use as indicators in order to capture what you perceive to be a type of market move that you want to exploit.

Filter/Screening: With thousands of instruments out there around the world, a trader needs to narrow down the field of possible candidates. This can be done with various broker screening tools, your favorite trading platforms, or simply by looking down lists of possible candidates and selecting the ones you wish to concentrate on trading.

Setup/Ranking: You probably still have too many candidates to trade at this point, so you may want to limit yourself to trading only candidates that have a special price action that makes them your trading target. This is where the ranking comes in to narrow the field of candidates for that day's trading. You now have your portfolio selection process complete for the next period.

Entry: You've got to have a Buy/Sell engine to trigger your action to get in. I call it an engine simply because it should "move" you to act. An engine moves a car. The Buy/Sell engine should move you.

Stop Loss: You should have a price at which you are going to cut this trade loose from the portfolio and admit it is not working out. Many traders do not believe in stop losses. They worry about the orders being taken advantage of and decide to use "mental stops." They rely on a preconceived idea about where they will get out instead of placing stop loss orders. I view this as a poor technique, since one mental stop can create a potential large loss that will wipe out any small inefficiencies caused by stops being run in the marketplace. Stop loss orders are a must to the All-Weather Trader.

Take Profit/Where You Are Exiting the Trade: If a strategy trades over only a few days, you can set the target by some logical method. For example, you might take profit at two times your risk on the trade. You might take profit on a short-term trade at a level where the market has achieved a "normal" level after being overbought or oversold. If a trade languishes and doesn't make it to your target, you could cut it loose so that you aren't tying up precious capital on a position that isn't working out. This would be referred to as a time stop. (As a specified time period elapses, you get out of the position.)

In longer-term trend-following strategies, you will target taking your profit when the trend falters and changes to the opposite direction. At that point you stop out of the trade, hopefully with a nice profit. The major point in this section is that you need to have a plan for exiting the trade. Having no exit plan equals buy and hold, and the All-Weather Trader does not want to put himself in that situation.

Position Sizing: After all the screening, sorting, and buying or selling work, you still have to figure out how to properly size your positions. Too much size and you risk blowing up the account. Too little size and the position will not have sufficient impact to the portfolio to make a difference.

Every trading strategy will have these same attributes. You might even have some additional characteristics like ranking the candidates you get, so that you pick the top X candidates each day. You might want to allow re-entry into the position if you get stopped out, but it comes up again as a candidate to trade. You should have a position-sizing strategy that is geared to work with what your strategy is attempting to achieve. I'll cover that more in Chapter 10.

The bottom line here is that you don't have to lock your thinking into one style of trading. You can have some strategies that exploit trends, some that protect you from catastrophes, some that mean revert, and others that might pick up time premiums on options. Some could trade in the stock market, others could use ETFs, and still others might diversify into futures contracts. Some might be extremely long-term, and others could be short-term. They all should contribute to improving returns or managing the risk that causes sleepless nights while keeping that equity curve as straight as possible.

5

TIMING INVESTMENTS

I CAN HEAR THE ROAR HERE IN SCOTTSDALE COMING in from every direction: "But isn't it true that timing doesn't work? That's what I've heard from the university professors, the financial planners, and the stockbrokers." I answer that with, "Depends on what your goals are in timing an investment."

This obsession with only the return side of the return-to-risk challenge has amazed me over the years. Buying and holding any investment for a lifetime is going to carry with it less transaction cost, less time spent in managing it, more returns when the market goes in your favor, and more losses when the market goes against you. The last item, the losses, is what gets everyone. I know that I, a seasoned veteran of trading, could never have the patience to stick around in an investment that is down 25 percent with no protection against it, producing even greater losses. If a trader with fifty years of trading experience can't do it, what are the odds that you can?

I recently updated a study that I did for a research paper on my website, enjoytheride.world. I took the S&P 500 Index data available on Yahoo Finance for free and created a simple ten- and forty-day moving average indicator to measure up or down direction shifts. I then labeled each signal Up, Down, or Sideways.

My target for an Up or Down move was for the index to move at least 5 percent. If a signal yielded less than 5 percent before that move ended with a new signal in the opposite direction, I deemed it a Sideways move. My goal was to get a sense of how much time the stock market spends in Up, Down, and Sideways action. I've included Graphic 10, a table of findings.

There are many important takeaways from those results. First, the stock market spends a heck of a lot of time going nowhere. More than 60.5% of the days are spent in sideways market conditions. Only 30.50% of days give you momentum in Up markets. Down periods constitute only 9.95% of time.

Down markets are usually faster moving than Up markets. Fear apparently motivates traders to act quickly. In Down markets you would have gained 12.91% compound growth rate for only 9.95% of the time. Up markets grind it out a bit more for 15.02% return 30.50% of the time. Quick math tells us that Down markets achieve 12.91%/15.02% = 85.95% of the movement of Up markets in 8.95%/30.50% = 29.34% of the elapsed time. When Down markets do occur, they can get ugly quickly.

The next thing you should take note of is the maximum drawdown percent. As we previously mentioned, most traders, including me, would not have the stomach to tolerate a -56.78 percent drawdown in the Buy and Hold strategy. Therefore, the strategy would likely be abandoned at some point, and the trader would never see the total Compound Annual Growth Rate indicated. Timing cut that drawdown in half, a much easier situation to tolerate.

GRAPHIC 10—SUMMARY OF TIMING VS. BUY AND HOLD, JAN 1964 TO DEC 2021 (58 YEARS)

	UP MKT	DOWN MKT	SIDEWAYS MKT	TOTAL	BUY & HOLD	TIMING
Number of Trades	34	16	379	429	1	429
% of Trades	7.93	3.73	88.34	100	100	100
Number of Days	6,348	1,862	12,606	20,816	20,816	20,816
% of Days	30.50	8.95	60.56	100	100	100
Compound Avg Growth %	510.62	206.56	-510.04	207.145	7.41	4.76
Avg % per Trade	15.02	12.91	-1.35			
Maximum Drawdown%					-56.7754	-25.3604
Return/ MaxDD					0.1305	0.1876

The last item I noticed was that the return for Timing is 64 percent of the return for Buy and Hold, while the Maximum Drawdown is less than half. Therefore, the return to maximum drawdown was 0.1305 for Buy and Hold versus 0.1876 for Timing, a 43.7 percent improvement in return-to-risk. This characteristic alone will tend to make the ride a lot easier over the decades and allow you more psychological room to stick with the strategy.

LET'S TIME THE S&P 500 INDEX

The SPY ETF is a highly liquid trading vehicle that attempts to match the Standard and Poor's 500 Index in an ETF format. I created a simple long using only three indicator Buy/Sell engines including Donchian, Keltner, and Bollinger Bands to trigger my trades. I invested 5 percent risk to equity in the SPY ETF on every buy signal and stayed in cash not earning any interest when in a down direction. The results are in Graphic 11.

Realizing that this is a simulation, and it earned no interest on the idle cash, the results show a historical positive return of +6.489 percent, decent return-to-risk ratios, a win rate of over 50 percent, and more than doubling of the equity in the twelve years. And, you had to do only thirty-four trades, about 2.7 trades per year on average. Fairly easy trading it seems to me.

Sim Trader

GRAPHIC 11—TIMING THE PRICE MOVEMENTS OF THE SPY ETF

- Period measured: January 1, 2010, to June 1, 2022 (12.41 years)
- $100,000 initial investment, 100% of equity on every new signal, long only
- Three-indicator timing package
- 21 days (Donchian 21-day; Keltner 21-day, 2.3 factor; Bollinger 21-day, 2.0 factor for buy trades, 50-day for sells)

STATISTIC	RESULT OF UP SIGNALS
Compound Average Growth Rate (CAGR%)	6.489
Sharpe Ratio	0.718
Sortino Ratio	0.889
Return to Average Drawdown	3.727
Return to Maximum (Drawdown)	0.375
Maximum Drawdown %	-17.316
Total Number of Trades (12.41 Years)	34
Winning Trades	18
Losing Trades	16
Win %	52.941
Profit Factor (Profit on Winning Trades/Loss on Losing Trades)	$2.68
Total Profits	$113,882

WHAT INVESTMENTS CAN YOU TIME?

You can time just about any market you decide has serious risk of loss in order to manage some of that risk. Timing is essentially attacking that risk by removing the risk from the portfolio in return for some tame money market–like investment. You are riding out the storm in a safe haven until it abates.

I started out my career timing mutual funds. I would run my indicators at the end of the day, see that I had a signal to buy or sell, and send a fax into the mutual fund desk to buy or sell the fund at the close. When exchange traded funds came into being, I started timing those instruments. Since then, I've timed Nasdaq Index futures, Bitcoin and Ethereum futures, and commodity, energy, currency, and metals markets.

The old saying goes, "You can't control the wind, but you can adjust your sails." That's such a great way of summing up timing. The market will do whatever, but you have control over your exposure to the risk. Timing is a simple, easy way to change your risk exposures dramatically.

Other Examples of Timing Crude Oil Futures

Anyone watching the business news over the last decade or two or filling up their car's gas tank at the pumps realizes that oil prices worldwide go up, and they go down. If you are running a business that must sell or consume oil or oil products, you know that the price movements can create profits or losses very quickly if prices move in your favor or against you. That sounds like a risk we ought to be able to attack. Let's think it through.

I took price data from the West Texas Intermediate Crude Oil contract trading on the New York Mercantile Exchange over the last X years and loaded it into SimTrader, a simulation and trading platform I use. I then set up a BUY/SELL indicator that was a combination of three indicators: Donchian Channels, Keltner Bands, and Bollinger Bands, which I'll explain when I list these as my three favorite indicators later in the chapter.

I selected a twenty-one-day period for the purpose of this study. This would not be too short term, which would yield a lot of trades and more trading costs. It would also not be so long term that it would be closer to a buy and hold strategy, doing little to attack the risk of price movement.

The results are about as expected. Assuming trading just a single contract of crude oil, the market spent a great deal of time in sideways action. Up- and Down-market periods were the most profitable as price movement equals risk, which is where the trader profits. It's really hard to produce significant profits in the market when prices do not go up or down. Up or Down periods are either potentiallly good or bad for all those businesses that include the cost of oil in their income statements.

Let's take the case of airlines that consume a lot of jet fuel, which of course comes from crude oil. If prices are rising, the cost of flying goes up, potentially reducing their profits if they can't pass that cost along to the passengers. Conversely, when the price of crude oil declines, the airlines have a less expensive fuel cost, and at the same ticket price, have more potential profits.

Sim Trader

GRAPHIC 12—TIMING THE PRICE MOVEMENTS IN CRUDE OIL

- Period measured: January 1, 2010, to June 1, 2022 (12.41 years)
- $100,000 initial investment, 100% of equity on every new signal, long only
- Three-indicator timing package
- 21 days (Donchian 21-day; Keltner 21-day, 2.3 factor; Bollinger 21-day, 2.0 factor for buy trades, 50-day for sells)

STATISTIC	RESULT OF UP SIGNALS	RESULT OF DOWN SIGNALS
Compound Average Growth Rate (CAGR%)	3.327	3.691
Sharpe Ratio	0.323	0.344
Sortino Ratio	0.436	0.508
Return to Average Drawdown	0.966	0.614
Return to Maximum Drawdown (MAR Ratio)	0.106	0.099
Maximum Drawdown %	-31.501	-37.354
Total Number of Trades (12.41 Years)	95	56
Winning Trades	44	17
Losing Trades	51	39
Win %	46.316	30.357
Profit Factor (Profit on Winning Trades/ Loss on Losing Trades)	1.34	1.42
Total Profits	$49,470	$53,910

Let's analyze the table. The airline could buy every Up trend of oil, meaning that as they lost some profit potential on their flying the plane, they would be making a profit on their futures contract. The results table shows that that would create $49,470 per contract of crude oil profits during those 12.4 years, many of which were tough on the airline industry. The Up signals that did not successfully result in a profit would be a loss or the cost of hedging. Those losses are included in the Up or Buy trades. So, had an airline run a hedging program concentrating on buying crude oil futures on Up direction indications and then sold and went unhedged during Down periods, their income statement's fluctuations would be lessened. They could concentrate more on running an efficient business, reassured those catastrophic losses due to huge moves up in their fuel costs would not hurt them badly.

They would also enjoy the benefit of the Down periods with lower potential costs of jet fuel. The table shows that the Sell trades on crude oil would have yielded $53,910 per contract of profits over the period. Those are periods that would have less expensive fuel costs and therefore less cost to get a plane up in the air. These periods would also serve to build up profits to help pay for times when the hedge didn't work out and produced a small loss.

Timing a Bond Exchange Traded Fund

Many businesses and individual traders are affected by interest rates and the yields on bonds increasing or decreasing. An individual bond investor will see the prices of bonds in his portfolio go down during periods of rapidly rising interest rates. He will conversely see the prices of bonds typically increase when interest rates and yield decline.

Businesses are affected as well. When interest rates decline, business cost of capital declines, making investment in new equipment cheaper and growth more possible. When interest rates move up, cost of capital increases, making it more expensive to expand the business. You can imagine that a mortgage company selling variable rate mortgages to homeowners would not enjoy rising interest rates because of the corresponding decline in the face value of their mortgage portfolio and the defaults that occur as homeowners struggle to pay higher interest rate payments. This looks like another possible use of timing to attack interest rate risks.

Let's use the same two-indicator set on a bond ETF to see what would happen if it had been timed over the last decade. I used a twenty-one-day period for the indicators in order to look at medium-term movements in the interest rate markets.

The previous table shows the results of buying or selling ticker symbol SCHQ, a long-term Treasury bond ETF. As you can see, Buy signals, indicating an Up period for bond prices and therefore lower yields on bonds, occurred frequently over this period as interest rates declined a fair amount.

In the period measured, a mortgage company would have the wind at its back. In a period when yields are declining, they might sell a pool of mortgages for more than they made in loans and book some extra profits. However, should the interest rates have a long period of increasing yield, the wind definitely will be in the face of debt holders, and creating profits from an investment helps to offset a bit of that risk, smoothing financial operations.

Sim Trader

GRAPHIC 13—TIMING THE PRICE MOVEMENTS IN A LONG-TERM TREASURY BOND ETF

- Period measured: January 1, 2010, to June 1, 2022 (12.41 years)
- $100,000 initial investment, 100% of equity on every new signal, long only
- Three-indicator timing package
- 21 days (Donchian 21-day; Keltner 21-day, 2.3 factor; Bollinger 21-day, 2.0 factor for buy trades, 50-day for sells)

STATISTIC	RESULT OF UP SIGNALS	RESULT OF DOWN SIGNALS
Compound Average Growth Rate (CAGR%)	1.328	0
Sharpe Ratio	0.126	
Sortino Ratio	0.168	0
Return to Average Drawdown	0.344	0
Return to Maximum Drawdown (MAR Ratio)	0.068	0
Maximum Drawdown %	-19.539	0
Total Number of Trades (12.41 Years)	7	0
Winning Trades	4	0
Losing Trades	3	0
Win %	57.143	0
Profit Factor (Profit on Winning Trades/ Loss on Losing Trades)	$1.38	0
Total Profits	$2,819	0

Sector ETF Timing

This is something that I've been doing for my own portfolio for decades in various formats. Many years ago, I timed sector mutual funds. With the advent of ETFs, and the ability to trade the position long or short, I moved to timing sector ETFs. So, I have extensive experience timing funds.

In my opinion, ETF timing is an excellent approach to handling smaller amounts of money. First of all, most brokerage firms have drastically reduced or even eliminated stock commissions. This allows you to buy extremely small amounts of shares without much negative consequence.

Second, any one ETF is a collection of stocks within the fund, spreading the risk of that one position over a number of companies' stocks. This helps to offset the effect of one company's bad earnings or an extraordinary news event that moves the stock by a massive percentage.

Third, ETFs come in a lot of flavors. Sector ETFs cover the range of various industries, capitalizations, market directions. Some are actively managed while others hold stocks in an index passively. Some are more expensive than others. It's like a candy store. You get to pick whatever candy you prefer.

I did not do an extensive screen on all the available ETFs in setting up my own sector ETF timing strategy. Most of the ETFs would be from the SPDR sector funds family you see advertised on the financial programs from time to time. Because I so often get the question, "What sector ETFs do you use?" I've listed their tickers and names below. As usual with everything in this book, any instruments, indicators, or parameters I use currently are subject to change as I grow my strategies as an All-Weather Trader.

GRAPHIC 14—LIST OF SECTOR ETFs THAT I CURRENTLY USE SUBJECT TO CHANGE

TICKER	NAME OF ETF
EEM	Ishares MSCI Emerging Market
GNR	SPDR Global Natural Resources
IWO	Ishares Russell 2000 Growth
JNK	SPDR High-Yield Bond
KBE	SPDR S&P Bank
KRE	SPDR Regional Banks
SPDW	SPDR Developed World, Ex-US Stocks
SPSM	SPDR S&P 600 Small-Cap Stocks
XAR	SPDR Aerospace & Defense
XBI	SPDR Biotech
XES	SPDR Oil & Gas Equipment & Services
XHB	SPDR S&P Homebuilders
XLB	SPDR Materials Select Sector
XLC	SPDR Communication Services
XLE	SPDR Energy Select Sector
XLF	SPDR Financial Select Sector
XLI	SPDR Industrial Select Sector
XLK	SPDR Technology Select Sector
XLP	SPDR Consumer Staples
XLU	SPDR Utilities Select Sector
XLV	SPDR Healthcare Select Sector
XLY	SPDR Consumer Discretionary Select Sector
XME	SPDR S&P Metals & Mining
XOP	SPDR Oil & Gas Exploration & Production
XPH	SPDR Pharmaceuticals
XRT	SPDR S&P Retail
XSD	SPDR S&P Semiconductor Sector
XSW	SPDR Software and Services
XTL	SPDR S&P Telecom
XTN	SPDR S&P Transportation

I have a portfolio of thirty different ETFs that each have market risk, so how might I make them more All-Weather? I time them, of course! Using the same three indicators that I will detail at the end of the chapter, I ran the data on these twenty funds over the same 12.4-year period used in the previous examples on the SimTrader platform.

Sim Trader

GRAPHIC 15—SECTOR ETF TIMING—LONG ONLY

- Period measured: January 1, 2010, to June 1, 2022 (12.41 years)
- $100,000 initial investment, 100% of equity on every new signal, long only
- Three-indicator timing package
- 21 days (Donchian 21-day; Keltner 21-day, 2.3 factor; Bollinger 21-day, 2.0 factor for buy trades, 50-day for sells)

STATISTIC	RESULT OF UP SIGNALS	RESULT OF DOWN SIGNALS
Compound Average Growth Rate (CAGR%)	24.043	0
Sharpe Ratio	0.849	
Sortino Ratio	1.110	0
Return to Average Drawdown	3.402	0
Return to Maximum Drawdown (MAR Ratio)	0.492	0
Maximum Drawdown %	-48.859	0
Total Number of Trades (12.41 Years)	1,048	0
Winning Trades	411	0
Losing Trades	607	0
Win %	42.080	0
Profit Factor (Profit on Winning Trades/ Loss on Losing Trades)	$1.50	0
Total Profits	$1,290,977	0

The results are very close to what I've experienced in the real world over time. The ETFs are long and very profitable during extended bull markets. We have had a lot of that over the last twelve-plus years. During extended bear markets, the ETFs go to cash and preserve assets. During sideways periods, timing can struggle, taking many small losses that can add up.

I'm exploiting positive risk when a sector goes into an up direction. I'm attacking negative risk of a down move in the sector. I'm trying to hold my own when markets are doing nothing. That adds up to All-Weather in my opinion.

WHAT TO LOOK FOR IN A TIMING CANDIDATE

Timing will only produce profits or avoid losses when markets move significantly. No movement means no profits or risk to deal with, so the first criterion you should look for is freedom of movement. The farther something moves, the better that timing vehicle will be.

The second criterion should be liquidity. Most trading instruments have what is called a bid/ask spread. The bid price is the highest price that a buyer is willing to pay for the item. The ask price is the lowest price that a seller is willing to sell the item for. If for a moment the price of the bid equals the price of the ask, a transaction happens, and both the buyer and the seller get their price.

Liquid markets with lots of trading volume will have the tightest bid/ask spreads and therefore the lowest cost of trading inefficiencies. Look for larger companies, markets with high volumes, and trading instruments that have exhibited tight bid/ask spreads in the past.

Another criterion to use in selecting timing candidates is high volatility. The faster an instrument moves, the more risk can be successfully embraced or managed. Many broker platforms will have historical volatility as one of the many criteria you can use to screen good timing candidates from the multitude of possibilities.

Leveraged/Inverse Exchange Traded Funds

Fund managers have created all sorts of ETFs that have very different exposures from the old mutual funds. You can now find funds that act like a triple-leveraged index fund or buy an inverse fund that produces a profit when the index that it is based on goes down. The leverage and direction flexibility of some of these new funds provides the trader who wants to time investments an opportunity to structure various aggressive positions, should they decide to use them. However, be careful with these. The costs may be higher to own them, and the leverage in some of them can get scary when the position is moving against you.

Timing an IRA/401K or
Tax-Deferred/Exempt Portfolio

What about the value of an investment inside of a tax-deferred or tax-exempt portfolio? I have had so many people tell me that they can't sell a position in a portfolio because "I'm down in value from where I bought it." This thinking is so misguided. Taxwise, there is very little consequence to buying or selling an investment inside the legal structure of an IRA, a 401K, a pension plan, or another tax-advantaged portfolio. This means that a dollar of cash is very nearly the same as a dollar of stock or a dollar of bonds or a dollar of anything. A couple of clicks on your computer and with very low transaction costs, you can move from one investment to another with zero tax consequences.

There is no logical reason that you should force yourself to stay in a losing position. The value of that in your portfolio is the price you need to consider. Where you bought it or when you bought it is nearly useless. Situating your positions in the portfolio to produce a profit or reduce a risk are the only things that matter.

Bottom line: Timing is a great way to attack risk inside some of these tax-advantaged portfolios since there are no tax consequences to creating realized gains or losses. A dollar is a dollar is a dollar inside of these portfolios.

TIMING INDICATORS TO CONSIDER

There are probably as many timing indicators and parameter sets as there are traders in the world. I call these indicators

Buy/Sell engines. Like the name implies, an engine is something that creates movement, and a Buy/Sell engine creates an action to buy or sell. So, what do I look for in a useful timing Buy/Sell engine? Let's look at some considerations.

First, I want to have something so simple that I could easily program a computer to calculate it each period. I should be able to easily describe the indicator's logic to someone and have him understand it. A simple Buy/Sell engine should leave absolutely no doubt about what to do: buy, sell, or nothing.

Also, I like indicators that have a minimum number of parameters. Jack Schwager, the author of the Wizard series about traders, is a successful trader in his own right. In a conversation I had with him, he used the phrase "degrees of restriction." He was referring to the concept that the more parameters you need to specify in an indicator, the more restrictive you make the indicator. With more parameters, the indicator will be less robust in dealing with various conditions it will face in the future. Therefore, I prefer indicators with few parameters.

Next, I prefer indicators that have a clear indication of market direction or lack thereof. I like indicators that include a noise zone where there is negligible normal price movement. Larger price movements can trigger Up or Down direction signals, giving the trader a clear sign to buy or sell, respectively. I am not a fan of moving averages, because there is no noise zone.

Lastly, I don't think it is really enjoyable or logical to have to periodically "optimize" an indicator or its parameters.

A fifty-day moving average may have only one parameter, which is great. However, fifty days may be optimal for creating signals one year and not even close to optimal the next year. I look for indicators that adjust to varying market conditions. If a market becomes more volatile, I want the indicator to automatically give me a wider noise band. In stable periods, I want tighter levels of price movement to trigger more timely signals.

THREE OF MY FAVORITE TREND-FOLLOWING INDICATORS

Donchian Channels Background

One of the simplest indicators that I've used for decades was created by Richard Donchian, whom I had the good fortune to listen to at a private dinner for traders a few decades ago. Donchian Channel is an indicator that now bears his name.

His theory was simple and the indicator easy to construct and use. He created a channel above and below normal price movement. He selected just one parameter, the number of periods he looked backward on in the price data.

Buy on the UP signal, sell on the DOWN signal, and the rest of the time do nothing. A Donchian Channel indicator is simple, has only one parameter, has a noise zone, and expands and contracts the noise zone when prices move farther in volatile periods and move less in quiet markets. It's a keeper.

DONCHIAN CHANNEL DEFINITION

Take the highest high of the last X days and the lowest low of the last X days and plot a channel above and below the price action to show the extremes of prices over the last X days. Between these extremes would be considered the noise zone and would be ignored. Above the high side of the channel, the trader could say that the market was in an uptrend. Below the bottom of the channel, one could see that the direction of the market was down. An advantage that Donchian Channels have is that they measure the farthest prices have strayed over the period specified.

Keltner Bands Background

Another good indicator is Keltner Bands. The Corporate Finance Institute describes the history of Keltner bands as this:

> The Keltner Channel is named after American grain trader Chester W. Keltner, who described it in his 1960 book entitled "How to Make Money in Commodities."

> Keltner initially described it as a ten-day moving average, and his initial version showed the center line showing the typical price, with it being the average of the high, low, and close (closing) price. The lines above and below the center-line were drawn at a distance away, with the said distance being the simple moving average of the past ten days' trading ranges.

Here, the overall strategy is to regard a closing price above the upper line as a strong bullish signal while a close below the lower line is bearish. The Keltner Channel was later further revised by Linda Bradford Raschke, who added in different averaging periods, an exponential moving average, and the average true range (ATR) for the bands.

KELTNER BANDS DEFINITION

This indicator starts with an exponential moving average, then adds a top and bottom line, based on volatility or ATR, to create a noise zone. So, a Keltner Band indicator is simple to calculate, has only two parameters (time and what multiples of ATR set the top and bottom band), has a noise band, and uses a measurement of volatility measurement (ATR) to expand or contract the top and bottom of the noise zone. It meets all my criteria for good indicators.

Keltner Bands also have a volatility component that adjusts on the fly when markets get more or less exciting. Volatility in this indicator is measured as Average True Range (ATR) over a period of X days. The indicator first calculates a moving average (I like exponential moving averages, but any will do), then adds or subtracts a multiple of ATR to or from the average. Picture three lines on the chart. The middle line will be the moving average, and that is likely to be in the middle of the price action or what I would call the noise. The top line would be a multiple of ATR (volatility) higher and therefore the top of the noise. The lower band would end up being the bottom of the noise.

Above the noise or top band, the market is in an uptrend. Below the bottom band, the market would be trending lower. Between the top and bottom would be noise and ignored.

Bollinger Bands Background

The final Buy/Sell engine I use is Bollinger Bands. John Bollinger, whom I met at a timing conference decades ago, created this indicator in the 1980s. This indicator arose from the need for adaptive trading bands and the observation that volatility is dynamic, not static, as was widely believed at the time.

Bollinger Bands can be applied in all the financial markets, including equities, forex, commodities, and futures. They can be used in most time frames, from very short-term periods to hourly, daily, weekly, or monthly.

BOLLINGER BANDS DEFINITION

This indicator is similar to Keltner Bands since it starts with an exponential moving average. However, Bollinger Bands use a measurement of volatility different from the one Keltners do: the standard deviation of prices over the last X number of periods. Like Keltners, Bollinger Bands use a factor to place a channel line above and below the noise zone. The standard deviation of prices is multiplied by the factor to calculate the high and low lines for the noise zone. Bollinger Bands are simple to calculate, have two parameters (time periods, factor), have a noise zone, and expand and contract the noise zone as the standard deviation of prices goes up or down, so this indicator rounds out the list of my three favorites.

TIMING SUMMARY

We've covered a lot in this chapter on how timing is a simple way to take on risk or reduce it by attacking it. I outlined three examples and show how with a simple set of indicators a trader can dramatically alter the risk landscape with a timing strategy. The general philosophy is to accept risk when the risk seems to be in your favor and attack risk when that risk would do damage.

It is not a perfect system. You will have periods when you get an indication of adverse risk, and the market quickly shrugs it off and resumes its march in your favor. Timing will create whipsaws, typically accompanied by small losses. This is the cost of timing and perfectly acceptable for use in my own portfolios. However, the important thing to remember is that in a period of extended price movement against you, using timing can mitigate a lot of the potential for major loss, and you can even profit from that risk in some instances. It is up to you as an All-Weather Trader to decide if the whipsaw losses are worth enjoying great periods of price movement and avoiding catastrophic losses.

6

HEDGING
YOUR PORTFOLIO

IN THE PREVIOUS CHAPTER WE LOOKED AT WAYS OF
timing a market to exploit risk for profit. When you set up a
timing program specifically to protect against a negative risk
to the rest of the portfolio, it would become a hedging strategy.
I use this approach in my equity portfolio. At any one time I
might own twenty-five to thirty different ETFs and an odd stock
or two, all generally long stock positions. Should a Down stock
market occur, those securities definitely will be swimming
upstream, so I use a hedging strategy to protect the portfolio in
addition to timing the individual long positions themselves as
we covered in the last chapter.

My portfolio tends to be quite diversified, but no matter what
you own long in the stock-oriented part of your portfolio, you
have to believe that should the stock market, as measured by
the popular indexes, decline by say 50 percent, your portfolio

will likely not have an easy time of it. Most portfolios would likely lose 40 to 60 percent if nothing were done to mitigate that risk.

Hedging is simply trying to create profits to offset losses. If my portfolio would likely lose a great deal during a long bear market, and I can create a profit to offset some of that, I've reduced risk and put myself at ease about the whole process.

MY OWN REAL-WORLD EXAMPLE

In my sector timing strategy, I look at twenty different sector ETFs and buy them on Up direction signals and sell them on Down indications. I rarely see all twenty funds yield Up signals, and I'm rarely totally in cash with this strategy. So, at any point in time, I do have some downside stock market risk that timing these ETFs has not taken care of. Therefore, I use an index hedging strategy to manage some of that risk.

First, I had to select my hedging vehicle. Since most of my ETFs cover the gamut of the entire stock market, I decided to use the S&P 500 stock index futures contract (Ticker Symbol ES) as a hedging vehicle. I thought that my risk of loss in the ETFs would likely come during Down stock market conditions, so I decided I should sell hedges on every indication of Down direction and buy back the hedge on every indication of an Up direction. With hedges off, my ETF portfolio would then be unbridled, and I could let the horses run.

The reasons I went with futures are many. First, I understand futures since I've traded them for over four decades. Second, current tax rules have gains/losses taxed at 60 percent long-term and 40 percent short-term capital gains. Lastly, wash sale rules don't apply here, so you can perform multiple hedges in a shorter period of time should you need to do so. I'm a trader, not a tax expert. However, I do think using futures for hedging my portfolio was a sound decision for me. You should consult your own tax expert for tax advice if you decide to use futures to hedge your portfolio.

Leaning on my study earlier of Up and Down periods, I noted that the stock market spends a lot more time in Up directions than Down. I decided to make use of that study and vary the sensitivity of the indicators depending on whether it was yielding an Up signal or Down. I made it harder for Down signals to trigger a hedge trade and made it easier to trigger a buy signal that would take off the hedges. I decided that for my portfolio, fifty days would be a suitable measurement period to trigger putting on the hedge trades, while only twenty-one days would be used for taking off the hedges. I used three indicators: Donchian Channel, Keltner Bands, and Bollinger Bands, and decided I would put the hedge in place on the first indicator that yielded a sell signal and would take it off on the first of the three indicators yielding a buy signal. The factor for the Keltner indicator I use currently is 2.3, and the factor for the Bollinger indicator is 2.0. All the parameter sets are shown in Graphic 16.

GRAPHIC 16—HEDGING PARAMETERS CURRENTLY IN USE, SUBJECT TO CHANGE

	DONCHIAN	KELTNER	BOLLINGER
▼ Down Direction Days	50	50	50
▼ Down Direction Factor	Not Applicable	2.3	2.0
▲ Up Direction Days	21	21	21
▲ Up Direction Factor	Not Applicable	2.3	2.0

Using these parameters and the SimTrader simulation platform, I tested Down signals only on the ES futures contract. I started with a simulated $10 million portfolio, so that none of the positions in the portfolio or the returns I received would be dependent on the size of the portfolio. Smaller portfolios will react in similar fashion to larger portfolios, but occasionally positions will drop out due to position-sizing algorithms creating a granularity in the results. **Using an excessively large amount of equity in the portfolio for simulations will give you more realistic results on what the logic and math you have created would have done for the period measured.** The stock market over the last few decades has generally been up, so hedging should have cost some, and it did. Up signals would have the portfolio picking up profits, and it did. The net result shown in Graphic 17 is that on balance, catastrophic downside risk of the portfolio was reduced, some measures of return-to-risk were improved, maximum drawdown was reduced as expected, and total profits were increased due to the positive effect of diversification, helping to increase the equity.

Sim Trader

GRAPHIC 17—ES HEDGE TIMING

- Period measured: January 1, 2010, to June 1, 2022 (12.41 years)
- $100,000 initial investment, 100% of equity on every new signal, long only
- Three-indicator timing package
- 21 days (Donchian 21-day; Keltner 21-day, 2.3 factor; Bollinger 21-day, 2.0 factor for buy trades, 50-day for sells)

STATISTIC	BUY AND HOLD	HEDGE ONLY	COMBINED
Compound Average Growth Rate (CAGR%)	11.960	-4.161	11.079
Sharpe Ratio	0.934	-0.453	1.013
Sortino Ratio	1.119	-0.655	1.275
Return to Average Drawdown	7.757	-0.695	6.812
Return to Maximum Drawdown (MAR Ratio)	0.396	-0.230	0.554
Maximum Drawdown %	-30.192	-18.090	-19.993
Total Number of Trades (12.41 Years)	1	9	29
Winning Trades	1	2	10
Losing Trades	0	7	19
Win %	100.000	22.222	34.483
Total Profits	$305,682	-$14,875	$267,832

A typical question that I get from traders running simulations is, "Why would I want to add the Hedge Only strategy when it loses money over the entire simulation?" The answer is that it helps to produce more predictable profits by smoothing the equity curve and avoids some of those catastrophic losses that require a very large return just to make back the losses. The trader can take the profits from a bear market hedge and buy more stocks at much lower prices, improving the return-to-risk ratios. The ability to compound and to keep the trader even-keeled mentally is far more important long-term than most traders realize. In my mind, it's so important, I would not consider being long stock without a hedging strategy in place for big, bad bear markets.

HOW MUCH SHOULD YOU HEDGE?

Now that we've got a plan to hedge the risk in the portfolio, we have to answer the question, "What size should the hedge be?" If you had a $100,000 diversified stock portfolio that was long ten different stocks in equal amounts of $10,000 each, how might we figure out how much of hedge we would need to protect ourselves in a bear market?

The simple, easiest way to calculate the answer is to make the hedge the same dollar amount as the portfolio's stock positions. So, a trader could sell $100,000 face value of index futures and realize that although the index will not move precisely like the stocks in the portfolio, the risk has been dramatically reduced.

The problem with this simplistic approach? You haven't considered the speed at which the portfolio and the hedge move and matched them up. By using just simple dollar amounts, you may have too much hedge on or not enough. A portfolio of utility stocks is going to move slower than the hedge. A portfolio of volatile tech stocks may move faster than the hedge. These examples will have the hedge mismatched to the portfolio. Even worse, you will not know which it is until the hedge trade is done and closed out.

A simple way to size a more effective hedge is to measure the volatility of the portfolio. Using a simple average percent movement per day over an appropriate period of time, you can determine how much of a hedge position will match the volatility of the stock portfolio. If you have the same $100,000 stock portfolio and over the last fifty days, the average percent move per day was 0.3 percent and the average percent movement per day in the hedge was 0.3 percent, then you would need $100,000 face value of hedge to match the portfolio. If, however, the hedge volatility was 0.15 percent, it would take twice as much hedge, or $200,000 face value, to match up with the portfolio.

WHAT SHOULD YOU USE TO HEDGE?

Not everyone has my knowledge or comfort level with trading futures as a hedge. Some stock brokerage firms do not even offer access to the futures markets, so traders need to assess their options when deciding what to use for their hedges. If your portfolio is at a brokerage firm that allows both stocks and futures, then you can follow the example above and use futures contracts with a trend-following indicator or set of indicators and hedge that way.

On the other hand, if your portfolio is sitting at a brokerage firm that does not give you access to futures, you may have to use other approaches to hedge your portfolio. If you have a margin account, you could short an index ETF that correlates well with your portfolio. For example, if you own mostly technology names in your portfolio, you might want to use a NASDAQ index ETF like ticker symbol QQQ and short it on Down moves, taking it off on Up moves.

I had a conversation with one trader who owned a portfolio of Pacific Rim stocks because he traveled frequently in that part of the world and felt comfortable owning stock in companies that he knew something about. He found a Pacific Rim index ETF that correlated well to the movement of his own portfolio and used that index ETF as his short vehicle to hedge the portfolio during Down moves. This is a perfect example of thinking through your hedging vehicle and matching it to your own portfolio.

In my wife's IRA, I had a different problem. Inside the IRA, I could not execute a short sale on an exchange traded fund due to IRS rules for IRAs. I solved the problem by buying long into a triple-leveraged inverse fund like ticker SPXU in an appropriate amount. That way, I had one more long position in the IRA, but the portfolio was still hedged.

FINDING YOUR OWN UNIQUE ALL-WEATHER HEDGING STRATEGY

I've covered a variety of ways you could consider hedging your portfolio. But because every reader of this book will have a different portfolio that needs hedging, each solution should be tailored to the hedging puzzle to be solved. Some of you might use a simple futures contract, while others may use an ETF or inverse ETF to reduce market risk in the portfolio.

To me, the important thing to realize is that it doesn't have to be perfect to take steps toward reducing the amount of pain that the portfolio and subsequently you will suffer. When you've measured that you are taking on more risk due to dangerous positions, adverse market movements, or impactful events coming up that will put you in harm's way, hedging your portfolio can go a long way to creating an All-Weather portfolio that can withstand the turbulence.

7

EXTREME DIVERSIFICATION

WHAT IS EXTREME DIVERSIFICATION?

IMAGINE THAT YOU ARE A MULTIBILLIONAIRE AND HAVE assets spread all over the world in different time zones, different markets, a huge futures portfolio where each position is long or short, real estate holdings, and currency positions. What would you expect a typical day to look like? You would see some profits in a percentage of all these investments and you would likely see some losses in the others. The net result: if the gains in the profitable positions are more than the unprofitable ones, your total portfolio has another positive day.

While most people reading this book (and the author) are not billionaires, we can still take advantage of some extreme diversification ideas and help ourselves out in smoothing our results. We may not be able to get to thousands of positions across the world, but the good news is that if we can even get to ten or twenty positions with very low correlation, we should see a less volatile portfolio.

WHAT IS CORRELATION AND WHY DO WE WANT TO KEEP IT LOW?

Correlation is a statistical concept measuring how much two items in a portfolio move like each other. If Stock A and Stock B are both very large companies in the energy business and the price of oil goes down 1 percent today, both stocks are likely to be negatively affected. If Stock A goes down by 0.75 percent for the day and Stock B goes down 0.75 percent, we can say these two stocks have a 100 percent correlation or a correlation coefficient of 1. This means that we are expecting these stocks to move exactly like each other. Correlation is usually measured over a period of many days.

It doesn't matter whether the price movements are up or down. If they move together, the correlation is 100 percent. But what would the correlation be if we had a stock portfolio that went down by 5 percent and a hedge, as discussed in the last chapter, that increased by 5 percent? These two items would be perfectly inversely correlated or have a correlation of -100 percent. The correlation coefficient would be -1. This is great for hedging since we are trying to offset potential losses in one part of the portfolio with profits from a hedge. However, this is not what we want in building an extremely diversified portfolio. Instruments like these would always be fighting each other and hurt the potential for profit.

We have to search for non-correlation or low correlation. Why? We want any two items in the diversified portfolio to do their own thing. One doesn't care what the other is doing, so both could be down, both could be up, or one could move in our direction and the other move against us. They are independent of each other. This helps to stabilize the portfolio overall and is one more tool the All-Weather Trader can use to smooth results.

Some Example Correlation Tables

When I started in the money management business, there were only a few ways to diversify your stock portfolio. You could buy stocks in different industries or in different countries. It wasn't ideal, but you could get some positive effects to the portfolio.

Today's fast-paced, electronics-driven economy makes the world a small place. If New York has a rough day, chances are that Sydney, Tokyo, Hong Kong, Paris, and London will all have bad days too. There is a lot less capability to diversify by country. Let's examine the long-term trends of stock correlations.

Below is a graph of the last century of Global Equity Market Correlations summarized nicely by Dennis P. Quinn and

Hans-Joachim Voth in their study on Global Correlations.[1] It clearly shows that the old ways of getting diversification are disappearing.

GRAPHIC 18—THE LAST CENTURY OF GLOBAL EQUITY MARKET CORRELATIONS

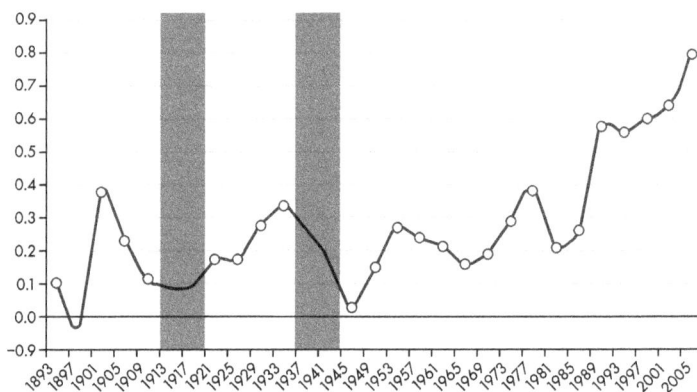

(Shaded areas indicate observations reflecting stock returns affected by the two world wars.)

Another example that clearly points out the lack of global diversification potential can be seen in a correlation matrix that I ran in June 2022. Any correlation above 0.80 would show very high correlation between the two markets shown on the X and Y axis of the table. Much lower correlations near 0.0 would show a lack of correlation and would be a place to diversify.

---

1 Dennis P. Quinn and Hans-Joachim Voth, "A Century of Global Equity Market Correlations," *American Economic Review* 98, no. 2 (2008): 535–540, http://www.aeaweb.org/articles.php?doi=10.1257/aer.98.2.535.

You can see that during the panic that most markets around the world are highly correlated and were acting in sync during what was a rough bear market period through the first half of 2022. During this period, and with these correlations, it would be hard to find a place to hide during this risky period.

GRAPHIC 19—WORLD STOCK MARKET CORRELATIONS

(COUNTRY)	R2000	NAS	S&P	NAS	DAX	CAC 40	SEOUL	ALL ORDS	NZSE	NIKKEI
Russell 2000 (US)	1	0.96	0.99	0.94	0.77	0.90	0.82	0.83	0.87	0.61
NASDAQ (US)	0.96	1	0.97	0.88	0.67	0.83	0.77	0.77	0.87	0.56
S&P 500 (US)	0.99	0.97	1	0.94	0.75	0.90	0.84	0.85	0.91	0.56
NASDAQ (UK)	0.94	0.88	0.94	1	0.82	0.92	0.87	0.90	0.86	0.60
DAX (Germany)	0.77	0.67	0.75	0.82	1	0.93	0.85	0.74	0.61	0.65
CAC 40 (France)	0.90	0.83	0.90	0.92	0.93	1	0.91	0.88	0.80	0.62
Seoul Comp (Korea)	0.82	0.77	0.84	0.87	0.85	0.91	1	0.91	0.84	0.45
All Ords (Australia)	0.83	0.77	0.85	0.90	0.74	0.88	0.91	1	0.92	0.48
NZSE (New Zealand)	0.87	0.87	0.91	0.86	0.61	0.80	0.84	0.92	1	0.44
NIKKEI 225 (Japan)	0.61	0.56	0.56	0.60	0.65	0.62	0.45	0.48	0.44	1

Recession Bear Market, June of 2022: https://www.macroaxis.com/invest/worldMarketCorrelation

You can see the lack of diversification in individual stocks as well. I saved two charts courtesy of McClellan Financial Publications (www.mcoscillator.com) and included them here. You can clearly see that when the stock market was getting hit hard in 2008, new lows on the New York Stock Exchange skyrocketed and new highs became nonexistent. What that means in simple terms is that most stocks were making new lows, and you had no place to hide if you owned a stock portfolio.

GRAPHIC 20—S&P 500 INDEX VS. NUMBER OF NYSE STOCKS AT NEW HIGHS & LOWS

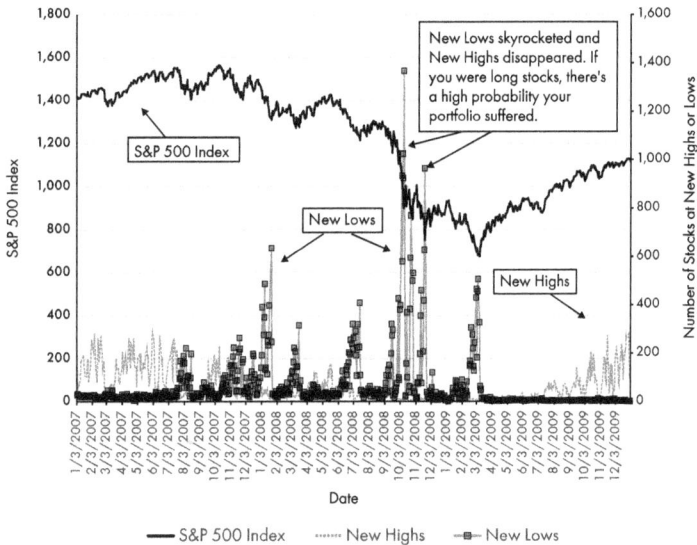

WHAT MARKETS ARE NON-CORRELATED?

I've spent a few pages driving home the point that 100 percent stock portfolios are getting very correlated. I would expect that during times of crisis, when panic tends to be reflected in the markets, a portfolio of 100 percent stocks will likely suffer. I decided back in the 1980s, as a long-only stock portfolio manager, that I needed to have something in my portfolio that might produce profits when the stock market went through one of its periodic catastrophic meltdowns. I wanted something that I could go long or short on and that was tax-efficient, liquid, and easy to trade. I looked at futures as having all these characteristics and set out to use them. Look at a matrix of various futures contracts and all the different correlations available to the trader from Moore Research Center, Inc. (www.mrci.com, telephone: 541-525-0521):

GRAPHIC 21—MRCI'S INTERMARKET CORRELATIONS (PREVIOUS 90 DAYS—FEBRUARY 14, 2022)

	YM	NQ	NK	US	ED	EU	JY	GC	PL	HG	CL	NG	KC	CC	SB	W	S	CT	LC	HE	LB
YM		73	70	23	9	4	-35	22	-4	3	-15	-18	-6	-24	8	10	-11	0	10	-32	7
NQ	73		80	73	45	-6	9	0	-30	-32	-70	-18	-10	-56	41	42	-55	-42	-7	-62	-24
NK	70	80		50	65	35	11	-25	14	-7	-47	21	-46	-22	64	28	-67	-44	-43	-69	-50
US	23	73	50		60	-5	53	-25	-42	-55	-89	-13	-21	-64	50	33	-73	-69	-26	-68	-41
ED	9	45	65	60		55	69	-36	8	-31	-65	49	-76	-14	76	3	-94	-77	-81	-85	-76
EU	4	-6	35	-5	55		42	-17	51	23	7	72	-79	42	37	-38	-42	-33	-64	-41	-55
JY	-35	9	11	53	69	42		-35	-5	-47	-52	37	-50	-2	57	0	-68	-60	-61	-52	-59
GC	22	0	-25	-25	-36	-17	-35		50	27	40	-18	26	6	-6	38	33	55	28	35	18
PL	-4	-30	14	-42	8	51	-5	50		45	56	62	-39	42	23	7	6	35	-23	17	-45
HG	3	-32	-7	-55	-31	23	-47	27	45		56	8	8	36	-30	-23	37	29	16	31	26
CL	-15	-70	-47	-89	-65	7	-52	40	56	56		18	19	59	-45	-25	76	81	35	73	32
NG	-18	-18	21	-13	49	72	37	-18	62	8	18		-68	39	41	-14	-32	-11	-53	-23	-74
KC	-6	-10	-46	-21	-76	-79	-50	26	-39	8	19	-68		-13	-52	26	64	50	79	61	70
CC	-24	-56	-22	-64	-14	42	-2	6	42	36	59	39	-13		4	-36	30	25	-5	34	5
SB	8	41	64	50	76	37	57	-6	23	-30	-45	41	-52	4		34	-75	-51	-55	-56	-72
W	10	42	28	33	3	-38	0	38	7	-23	-25	-14	26	-36	34		-15	10	17	-1	-29
S	-11	-55	-67	-73	-94	-42	-68	33	6	37	76	-32	64	30	-75	-15		84	77	90	69
CT	0	-42	-44	-69	-77	-33	-60	55	35	29	81	-11	50	25	-51	10	84		63	81	41
LC	10	-7	-43	-26	-81	-64	-61	28	-23	16	35	-53	79	-5	-55	17	77	63		72	63
HE	-32	-62	-69	-68	-85	-41	-52	35	17	31	73	-23	61	34	-56	-1	90	81	72		52
LB	7	-24	-50	-41	-76	-55	-59	18	-45	26	32	-74	70	5	-72	-29	69	41	63	52	

CODE FOR TICKERS:

YM = Dow Jones 30	GC = Gold	SB = Sugar
NQ = NASDAQ Index	PL = Platinum	W = Wheat
NK = Nikkei Index	HG = Copper	S = Soybeans
US = US Treasury 30-Year Bonds	CL = Crude Oil (West Texas)	CT = Cotton
ED = Eurodollar	NG = Natural Gas	LC = Live Cattle
EU = Eurodollar FX	KC = Coffee	HE = Hogs
JY = Japanese Yen	CC = Cocoa	LB = Lumber

Code for tickers:

YM = Dow Jones 30	NG = Natural Gas
NQ = NASDAQ index	KC = Coffee
NK = Nikkei Index	CC = Cocoa
US = US Treasury 30 Year Bonds	SB = Sugar
ED = Eurodollar	W = Wheat
EU = Eurodollar FX	S = Soybeans
JY = Japanese Yen	CT = Cotton
GC = Gold	LC = Live Cattle
PL= Platinum	HE = Hogs
HG = Copper	LB = Lumber
CL = Crude Oil (West Texas)	

The shaded squares are correlations that are either very positive or very negative. With high positive correlations, you are not getting much diversification. With high negative correlations, positions in your portfolio are potentially fighting each other. The shaded numbers are either greater than or equal to 80 or less than or equal to -80. These were not good diversifications over the ninety days measured by Moore Research. However, look at the table in its entirety and you see the vast majority of pairs are not highly correlated positive or negative. You can see lots of instrument pairs between -0.5 and 0.5, the non-correlated zone.

It makes sense, doesn't it? Why in the world would lumber prices care about what hogs are doing? Would Japanese yen traders care about cotton prices? Probably not. So, these markets with low correlations can move to the beat of their own drummer and can provide very different return streams to stabilize the portfolio. Reminds me of the old cutaway of an auto engine.

Each piston is in a different position at any moment in time, some high, some low, but all doing their job to turn the shaft and move the car forward. In the case of extreme diversification, if all the possible diversified positions have a positive chance of producing a profit, but do so at various times, the overall profit stream is likely to be steadier.

Using these non-correlated instruments, a trader can get closer to that magic diversified portfolio that has instruments that truly act on their own and are not tied to what something else in the portfolio is doing at that moment. It took me four years of trading small sizes of futures contracts to figure out what I wanted to do with them and to produce a profit, but when I arrived at that destination, it opened a whole new world of extreme diversification. It's a very nice destination, indeed!

Here's a real-world example from my Registered Commodity Trading Advisor (CTA) days at Trendstat Capital. The managed futures industry has to extract returns from the futures market, so it stands to reason that when futures markets are moving, there's profit to be had, and when markets are listless, CTAs tend to have a rough time. These profitable and unprofitable periods are not necessarily correlated with whatever stocks happen to be doing that period.

Here's a chart, courtesy of Barclay Hedge (www.barclayhedge. com), that tracks all sorts of interesting indices on the hedge fund and CTA industries. I used the Barclay CTA Index, which is defined on their website as follows.

> The Barclay CTA Index measures the composite performance of established programs. For purposes of this index, an established trading program is a trading program that has four years or more documented performance history. Once a trading program passes this four-year hurdle, its subsequent performance is included in this equally weighted and rebalanced at the beginning of each year index. The Barclay Index does not represent an actual portfolio, which could be invested in, and therefore the index performance results should be deemed to be hypothetical in nature and of comparative value only.

I plotted the CTA Index against the Standard & Poor's 500 Stock Index. Imagine creating a portfolio where you have 50

percent in stocks as measured by the S&P 500 Index and the
rest in the CTA Index as a proxy for a futures portfolio. As
you can see from the chart, there are several times in history
when the CTA index helps the performance and some when it
hurts the performance. That is another way of saying they are
non-correlated, which is what we are looking for in extreme
diversification.

GRAPHIC 23—RETURNS FROM CTAs AND S&P 500 COMBINED 50%/50%

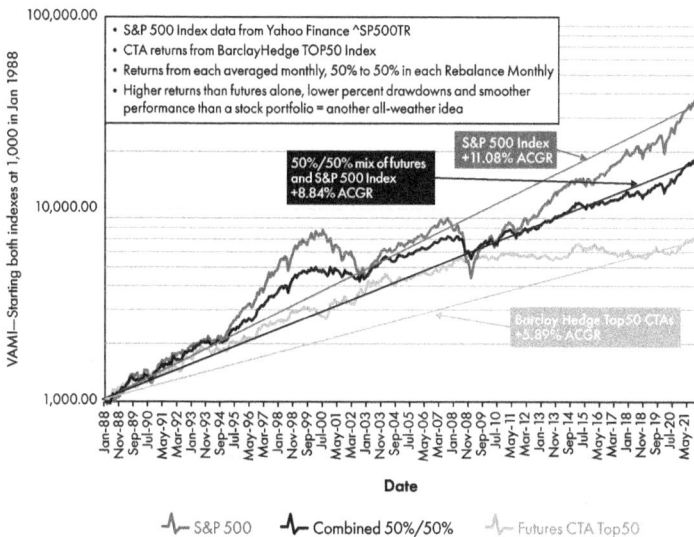

- S&P 500 Index data from Yahoo Finance ^SP500TR
- CTA returns from BarclayHedge TOP50 Index
- Returns from each averaged monthly, 50% to 50% in each Rebalance Monthly
- Higher returns than futures alone, lower percent drawdowns and smoother performance than a stock portfolio = another all-weather idea

50%/50% mix of futures and S&P 500 Index +8.84% ACGR

S&P 500 Index +11.08% ACGR

Barclay Hedge Top50 CTAs +5.89% ACGR

VAMI—Starting both indexes at 1,000 in Jan 1988

Date

⎼⋀⎼ S&P 500   ⎼⋀⎼ Combined 50%/50%   ⎼⋀⎼ Futures CTA Top50

BUT FUTURES ARE DANGEROUS, AREN'T THEY?

I get this question all the time, and despite my reputation as a
conservative trader, I have traded futures for about forty-five

years now. The key to using futures to diversify your portfolio lies in the use of leverage. While more leverage is dangerous, low leverage can be almost boring.

For example, let's take one mini contract of Crude Oil (West Texas Intermediate) trading on the Chicago Mercantile Exchange (CME) based on the large crude oil contract traded on the New York Mercantile Exchange (NYMEX.) This mini contract is for 500 barrels of crude oil for delivery at a future date. Say the price is $90/barrel. That means that a trader can buy $45,000 of crude oil at face value.

Now if you want to make it extremely dangerous, you put up the $4,200 that the CME requires as initial margin, and you own the crude oil at a 10.7-to-1 leverage, which is very dangerous indeed. If you went to the other extreme and paid full cash for the contract, you would put up $45,000, have zero leverage, and a somewhat boring position in your portfolio. The place where most traders would operate is somewhere in between. You would have some leverage, but not too much.

Think of real estate. Many real estate purchases are made with 10 to 20 percent down on the mortgage. Some are for full cash with no mortgage. Still others, especially back in the early 2000s, were with no money down. If you pay cash for the house, and continue to live there, it's a pretty boring part of your overall portfolio. If you put 5 percent down, fluctuations in real estate prices can quickly take you underwater on your mortgage. You have a negative equity left in the house after paying off the mortgage due to market fluctuations. A large part of managing the risk becomes managing the leverage.

Futures Margins—Not the Same as Stock Margins

The Federal Reserve (FED) sets the margin rates for stocks, which are at 50 percent at the time I am writing this book. Brokerage firms can set their own margin rates as long as they are at least as restrictive as the FED's margin rules.

In a securities portfolio, the broker is essentially lending you 100 percent of the value of your portfolio, allowing you to buy or sell additional positions beyond the cash value of your equity. The broker will charge you a short-term interest rate on the margin loan. Because a futures contract is simply an amount of something to be delivered or received at a future date, margin takes on a different meaning. It is basically a good-faith deposit to give your broker and the exchanges the assurance that you have the financial capacity to follow through on the promises you made in buying or selling the futures contract. In the crude oil example above, the exchange felt that $4,200 was a sufficient amount to provide those assurances.

Margins levels in futures can change dramatically. When markets go completely bonkers, exchanges can require increased amounts of "good-faith money" to reduce the leverage and calm the price movements. When markets are very stable for long periods of time, exchanges can lower the margin requirement to help increase the ability of traders to participate in that market.

Back in my CTA days at Trendstat, we operated around 15 to 20 percent of equity on our margin utilization. That means that we were at about 5-to-1 leverage on our average position. I'm at those levels today in my retirement portfolio, around 15 to 17 percent. The point I am making here is that you can set your own level of exposure wherever you want it. Running at higher margin-to-equity levels will be more exciting, and running with less leverage will make it easier mentally but will have less of an effect on the portfolio. You are your own All-Weather Trader. You get to decide where to dial it in.

Many smaller traders reading this book will point out that they don't feel comfortable with buying $45,000 worth of crude oil in their portfolio as in the example above. However, doing the math, a $1 move in $90/barrel crude is like having a stock that moves 1.1 percent for the day. There are a lot of tech stocks that move like that every day. The micro contracts have been coming to the marketplace in many futures markets, and I use them extensively. The CME has been particularly good at creating and trading micros on energy, cryptos, precious metals, stock indices, and other commodity sectors (https://www.cmegroup. com/markets/microsuite.html).

Diversifying by Time Period

For my own portfolio, I prefer an intermediate-term time period to run my positions in futures. I'm retired and don't wish to sit in front of a computer all day looking at prices meandering around. I make my decisions and ship my orders once per day and that's the only time I really need to look at the screen. The rest of the day I would rather be doing something more productive and enjoyable.

Some of you will want more action, and you can get it with time period diversification. Say you had a favorite Buy/Sell engine/ indicator that operated at twenty-one days or approximately one month of trading days. You could add another indicator that operated on nine days or some other shorter time period. The shorter term the indicator, the more trades you will be executing in the strategy. Fewer days in the indicator will also typically decrease the risk per contract to your stop loss levels. This may take more effort in managing your portfolio, but it can definitely be worth the extra effort in smoothing results and adding risk mitigation to your All-Weather portfolio.

Futures Overlay on Your Stock Portfolio

A concept that evolved back in the 1990s and 2000s, as I was retiring from full-time professional money management duties, was overlaying a managed futures strategy on top of a stock portfolio. If you think about it, for a $100,000 stock account, you are allowed to buy $200,000 of stocks in your portfolio. That leverages you, makes the risk of problems greater, and does little to diversify the portfolio. It usually is just a way of trying to jack up your returns on the portfolio.

How about if we took maybe 20 percent of the equity, or $20,000, and used it to diversify into a small, diversified portfolio of micro futures managed with a different strategy with a different time period used for the indicators? We would be trading a futures strategy at an equity of $100,000 but using only 15 to 20 percent of the available purchasing power in the account to cover the "good-faith" deposits of margin for the broker and exchanges to be happy. That still leaves us $80,000 in purchasing power untouched. We now have a $100,000 stock portfolio and, at the same time, using the same equity, we have the money working twice as hard in some diversified markets that are not tied to each other. We are "overlaying" the futures portfolio and its positions with the stock portfolio.

I have used this technique in my own trading for over twenty years now. I have seen it help diversify my portfolio, keep it more stable, provide some exciting returns when some futures markets go crazy, and maintain a more efficient use of my capital. Think of it as diversification by strategy. I'm running two strategies with more diversification with the same equity.

Let's do a hypothetical study of combining futures as measured by the Barclay Hedge Top 50 CTA Index with the S&P 500 Index representing stocks over the last thirty-four years. However, this time we're going to work the capital a little harder by overlaying the futures on top of the stock portfolio. I'm assuming margin is allowed in this case with 100 percent of the equity being used for the stocks and somewhere around 20–25 percent used in margin for the futures positions. I'm taking a liberty with the simple study by rebalancing, and margin interest costs are not included. Here's the graphical overview:

You can see that working the money twice as hard was beneficial, but the more important point is the overlay was more stable than the S&P 500 Index. More return and stability is exactly what this All-Weather Trader strives for.

GRAPHIC 24—EXAMPLE OF A FUTURES OVERLAY ON STOCKS

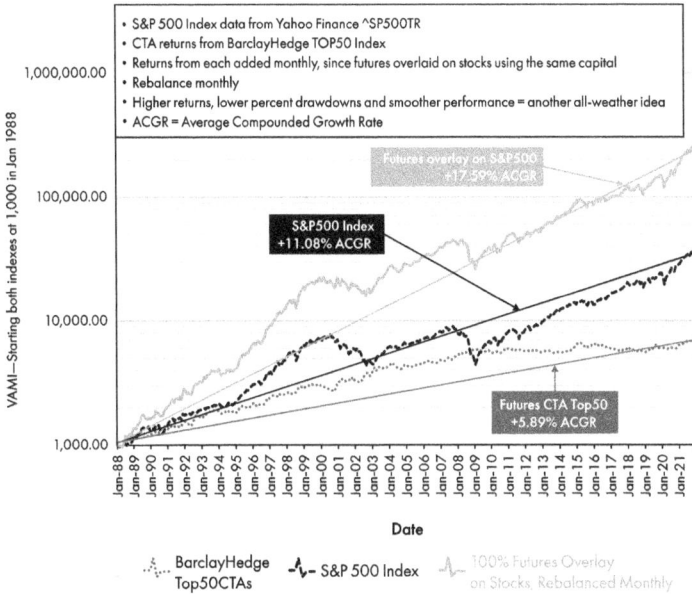

- S&P 500 Index data from Yahoo Finance ^SP500TR
- CTA returns from BarclayHedge TOP50 Index
- Returns from each added monthly, since futures overlaid on stocks using the same capital
- Rebalance monthly
- Higher returns, lower percent drawdowns and smoother performance = another all-weather idea
- ACGR = Average Compounded Growth Rate

Futures overlay on S&P500
+17.59% ACGR

S&P500 Index
+11.08% ACGR

Futures CTA Top50
+5.89% ACGR

VAMI—Starting both indexes at 1,000 in Jan 1988

Date

BarclayHedge Top50CTAs   S&P 500 Index   100% Futures Overlay on Stocks, Rebalanced Monthly

8

SIDEWAYS MARKETS— WHAT IF THE MARKETS GO NOWHERE?

IN PREVIOUS CHAPTERS I HAVE THROWN OUT IDEAS FOR trading using various markets, time frames, and strategies. However, everything I mentioned would tend to perform better when markets were going either up or down. The challenge to the All-Weather Trader is now what he would do in a sideways market. If you mathematically have to buy low, sell high or sell high and buy low in order to be able to produce a profit, in sideways markets you will struggle. Traders need market movement to produce reasonable returns.

In this chapter, I will give you some ideas that I've used for markets that are stuck going sideways for a while.

SIDEWAYS PERIODS CAN CREATE DRAWDOWNS

If you look at a performance graph of typical futures trading or ETF timing strategy, you will find that most drawdown periods are caused by price actions that create a lot of buys and sells, most of them at small losses. The trades just never run in your favor far enough to get to profitability.

GRAPHIC 25—EXAMPLE OF A FUTURES OVERLAY ON STOCKS

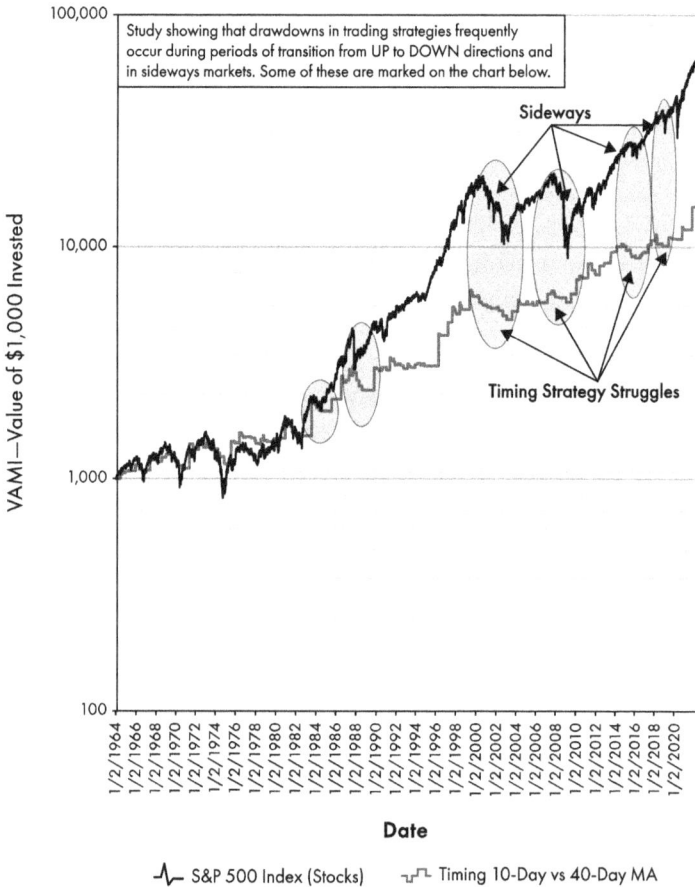

Study showing that drawdowns in trading strategies frequently occur during periods of transition from UP to DOWN directions and in sideways markets. Some of these are marked on the chart below.

S&P 500 Index (Stocks)　　　Timing 10-Day vs 40-Day MA

Trend following buys when the trend is moving higher and sells when the price movements are moving lower. In sideways markets, this can lead to whipsaws where the trader ends up buying and selling, typically at smaller losses, multiple times in a row. Enough of these happening across enough markets and you have yourself a nice little drawdown that's a mental drag.

I took a simple timing strategy and plotted it below using the S&P 500 Index timed with a ten-day and forty-moving average crossover indicator. You can see where I marked that these strategies will struggle when the instrument traded changes direction a lot or is basically sideways with its price movement.

NOISE IN THE MARKETS

In a previous chapter we showed that stocks have spent roughly 60 percent of their time going sideways over the last fifty-eight years. That means that more than half the time you spend in the stock market, you are going nowhere. During these periods, timing strategies tend to have choppy performance. Once again, if there's not much price movement, it's hard to buy low and sell high in a way that will produce large profits.

However, there will always be periods when the market runs up, approaches new highs, and gets overbought only to run out of steam and fall back into the sideways noise. On the other side of things, there are times when you're in the noise and prices get scary weak and traders start to think that the market is going to take another dip down only to watch it find its footing and rally back into the noise.

These smaller swings from overbought to oversold can be measured by various indicators. Oscillators are the best tool for this purpose; they rate where the market is right now compared with where it has been over the last X periods, normalized between 0 and 100. One hundred would be extremely over-bought and would warn of the potential to snap back lower. The opposite, a 0 reading, would be very oversold, warning of a possible rebound to the upside. Tack on your favorite Buy/Sell engine using a shorter-term time frame and you've got a strat-egy that could have some decent profits when prices are gener-ally moving sideways.

In Graphic 26 I have taken a six-month chart of Japanese Yen futures continuous contract. For the overbought/oversold indicator, I used a Stochastic RSI, a popular oscillator. I used a twenty-one-day period (about one month of trading days) to measure the condition. A simple Buy/Sell trigger like exceeding the previous day's extreme price in the direction of the warn-ing and stopping out using a very short-term trend-following model should give you the opportunity to get into short-term reversals and pick up small profits in those sideways periods.

Occasionally, you'll get lucky and jump into a longer run that turns into the next big move. You will be in early on the move. The reliability of these strategies will get to somewhere above 50 percent, and the average profit will approximate the average loss. I wouldn't want to trade this type of strategy all by itself. During strong bull or bear moves, the losing trades will come in a steady stream, trying your patience. But during those peri-ods I am typically slaying it with my trend-following models, so I give a little up on the big moves to have some strategies that can keep the portfolio stable during those periods when I know my trend-following models will struggle. It's all about smoothing out that equity curve and being able to handle all kinds of weather in the markets.

GRAPHIC 26—OVERBOUGHT/OVERSOLD CONDITIONS USING AN OSCILLATOR

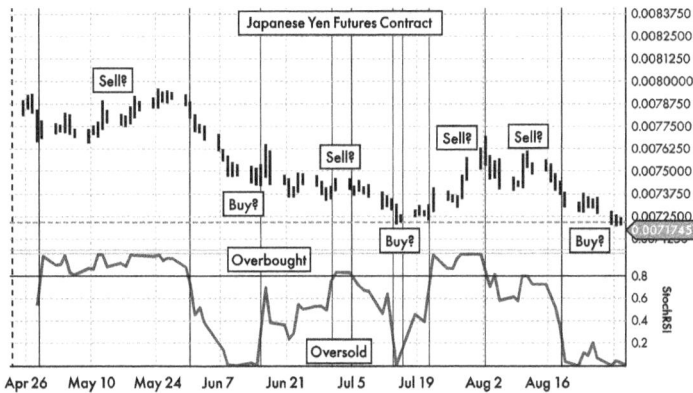

OPTION SPREADS

As soon as investors start talking about options, I am on my guard. I have found the data on options sketchy and the investment strategies less automatable, so most of my trading life I have stayed away. I'm not interested in the Greek alphabet and am not as tuned into deltas and gammas as I perhaps should be.

However, in the last couple of years I have found a simple way to use options that seems to pick up some profits when the stock market is going nowhere. In an earlier chapter, I presented the study on time spent in up, down, and sideways markets. Since I know that my trend following will struggle to make large profits in sideways markets and those periods are 60 percent of the time, it stands to reason if I could come up with a simple risk-limited approach to profiting during those periods, I'd stabilize the overall portfolio.

And it has done exactly that. Here's what I do. I take an oscillator to measure whether the market is overbought or oversold. I use the Stochastic RSI, but most of them would work in similar fashion. Pick your favorite. Then, when the market is overbought, I sell a credit call spread on the stock index for six to eight days out. Because it is a "credit" spread, I get paid for the position when I put it in place. If the market does indeed go sideways over the next X days until expiration, I keep the credit received. If the stock index goes against me four or five points, I lose a predefined amount of money. If it moves in my favor, the credit goes to zero value even quicker, and I sometimes close it out for pennies and put on another credit spread if the oscillator signals an overbought or oversold condition.

GRAPHIC 27—SUMMARY OF BULL AND BEAR SPREADS

OPTION STRATEGY	TRADE SETUP	STRIKE ORDER	STRATEGY RISK/REWARD	PROFITABLE CONDITIONS
Bull Put Spread	Sell Put/ Buy Put	Sell Higher/ Buy Lower	Limited Loss/ Limited Profit	Neutral, Bullish, Moderately Bearish
Bear Call Spread	Sell Call/ Buy Call	Sell Lower/ Buy Higher	Limited Loss/ Limited Profit	Neutral, Bearish, Moderately Bullish

Source: Investopedia

Here's a trade profile of what happens at various prices assuming you initiate the credit spread to the upside in an oversold condition. The index happens to be at 425, so I sell a 425 put and buy a 420 put. Notice that the profits *and* losses are limited in this strategy. Unlike trend following, where you would have a reliability below 40 percent and a positive, lopsided average profit to average loss ratio, in this strategy you are shooting for a reliability above 50 percent and more like a 1:1 average profit to average loss ratio.

GRAPHIC 28—SUMMARY OF VARIOUS OUTCOMES FOR AN EXAMPLE CREDIT SPREAD

SPY PRICE	425 PUT PRICE	420 PUT PRICE	TOTAL COST $	END $	NET $
426	0	0	-2.78	+0.00	+2.78
425	0	0	-2.78	+0.00	+2.78
424	1	0	-2.78	+1.00	+1.78
423	2	0	-2.78	+2.00	+0.78
422	3	0	-2.78	+3.00	-0.22
421	4	0	-2.78	+4.00	-1.22
420	5	0	-2.78	+5.00	-2.22
419	6	1	-2.78	+5.00	-2.22

It's a simple strategy that takes me a few minutes once or twice per week at the most. It has had a fairly high reliability ratio of gainers to losers. It generally picks up profits when I know my other strategies will struggle. That's why it's a perfect strategy for an All-Weather portfolio.

MEAN REVERSION

This is a strategy that many traders use for sideways markets. I do not use any true mean reversion because it can be time-consuming, but I may add it as automation permits. The essence of this type of strategy is that markets, especially when going sideways, are in a range trading mode. This allows the traders to buy at the bottom of the range and sell at the top. Even though I don't currently use them, these strategies can be useful in minimizing drawdowns caused by typical trend-following strategies.

With full credit to my friend, Laurens Bensdorp of the Trading Mastery School, here's a simple example of how you might construct a mean reversion strategy. He covers this in more detail in his best-selling book, *Automated Stock Trading Systems*, one of the best, easy-to-read practical books that I've ever read on multiple systems trading.

Objective: To buy stocks in an uptrend, have a significant sell-off, buy them, and watch them revert to their mean or normal price.

Belief: You are assuming that the stock has been strong in the past, has taken a breather, and will continue the uptrend.

Trading Universe: All stocks traded on the NYSE, AMEX, and NASDAQ exchanges. It is important to understand this would be a low expectancy strategy, thus a large trading universe is required so you get enough trading frequency to come through the process.

Filter:

- Average daily volume over the last fifty days of at least 500,000 shares, so that the stock has enough liquidity.

- Average dollar volume of at least $2.5 million over the last fifty trading days, another liquidity measure

- Average True Range greater than 4 percent. You want to have a stock that moves fast, so that you can get back to the mean quickly and take your profit, should one exist.

Setup:

- Close above the 100-day simple moving average plus one Average True Range of the last ten days. This measures a significant uptrend in the stock.

- Seven-day ADX (measures the strength of the move). Definitions on math on many broker platforms (or Investopedia.com) greater than fifty-five showing better-than-average strength of movement.

Ranking: Highest to lowest seven-day ADX, so you are concentrating on the stocks showing the most strength as measured by the ADX indicator.

Entry: Buy 3 percent below the previous close. The trader is trying to "steal" this good stock at an even better price and hope it finds its footing and quickly rallies back to the mean.

Stop Loss: Three Average True Ranges of the last ten days below the execution price. It's a volatile stock, and we need to give it room to start the reversion process.

Profit Taking:

- One Average True Range of the last ten days, or

- Time-based: After six days, if not stopped out or profits achieved, exit next day on open at market. Clearly at this point, the trade is not working out in your favor.

Now, I just copied Laurens' exact strategy outlined in his book as an example. There are thousands of ways of putting together a mean reverting strategy, but I wanted to show you this one, because it includes all the basics of a sound strategy.

COUNTER-TREND TRADING

I personally find it difficult to do "pure" mean reversion trading. I feel uncomfortable personally with putting a limit order at a market extreme, limiting my losses to an arbitrary point where prices have not yet traveled and basically betting that the market will turn and revert to the mean. It does that sometimes and sometimes it does not, particularly in very solid up or down markets. I hate to predict what the market will do, and mean reversion has a bit of predicting associated with it.

Counter-Trend Trading is a sort of cousin to Mean Reversion. It has many of the same attributes as Mean Reversion:

1. It seeks to profit from very short reversals against the long-term trend.

2. It has specific buy/sell points to get into the position and limit risk.

3. It uses overbought and oversold conditions to set up the trades.

4. It is not going to do very well if the long-term trend is strong and continues.

Let's get into what I consider to be Counter-Trend Trading. I look at overbought/oversold conditions and set up the trade in the opposite direction. If conditions on whatever oscillator I use indicate that the market is oversold after falling significantly, then I'm looking to buy. I then use an extremely short-term Buy/Sell engine to trigger a trend-following trade to the upside. I place my stop at the indicators in the opposite direction.

The time periods are different from my long-term trend-following timing models. When looking to capture very long-term trends in something like my Sector ETF Timing, I use fifty days for my sell stops and twenty-one days for my buy stops. In Counter-Trend Trading, I would opt for something between one and three days, depending on whether it is in the futures markets or the stock markets. You can dial it in wherever you wish, but the important point is to make it a lot shorter time period than longer-term trend-following models you might have in the portfolio. You want to pick up profits in the sideways, so trades are going to be shorter, profit-to-loss ratios smaller, and trades a lot more frequent.

Because the profit-to-loss ratio of Counter-Trend models is lower than typical long-term trend-following models, you'll expect a higher profit/loss reliability percent on the trades. You should be striving for more than 50 percent on these types of strategies, but smaller profits on positive trades. A trick I've learned to use is to put on a normal position, then liquidate half of the position at a profit equal to the risk on the trade. In this way, that trade immediately becomes a low-risk trade, and the remaining position can be allowed to run like a typical trend-following trade, albeit for what will likely be a shorter time period.

Several things you can note looking at the statistics on these runs. First, let's remember that the same exact portfolio was used in the case of both the long-term and short-term strategies. Also keep in mind that the same three indicator package of Donchian, Keltner, and Bollinger was used in both cases. Normally, in the real world, I might mix up the indicators a bit to diversify by indicator, but I didn't in these cases to show some simple concepts. The number of trades in the short-term simulation is off the chart at 19,750 trades over the period. That would be a lot of work to keep up with and probably is not easy for many traders out there, but I wanted to show you how blending in something like this different short-term strategy can provide some diversification to longer-term strategies.

Sim Trader

GRAPHIC 29—EXTREMELY SHORT-TERM TIMING 26 LIQUID FUTURES MARKETS AND LONG-TERM TIMING, COMBINED

- Period measured: January 1, 2010, to June 1, 2022 (12.41 years)
- Short-term strategy specifications:
  - $10,000,000 0.1% of equity initial risk invested on each trade, 0.2% of equity ongoing risk invested for existing positions
  - Three-indicator timing package, 3 days
- Long-term strategy specifications:
  - $10,000,000 0.5% of equity initial risk and 0.2% of equity initial volatility invested on each trade, 1.0% risk and 0.5% volatility limits on ongoing trades; maximum portfolio risk of 15%, maximum portfolio volatility of 7%
  - Three-indicator timing package, 21 days
- Combined strategies:
  - 100% of equity targeted for both strategies, rebalanced continually

STATISTIC	SHORT-TERM RESULT	LONG-TERM RESULT	COMBINED RESULT
Compound Average Growth Rate (CAGR%)	15.121	3.467	18.954
Sharpe Ratio	1.563	0.343	1.187
Sortino Ratio	2.360	0.556	2.000
Return to Average Drawdown	8.730	0.700	4.835
Return to Maximum Drawdown (MAR Ratio)	1.102	0.083	0.520
Maximum Drawdown %	-13.720	-41.770	-36.462
Total Number of Trades (12.41 Years)	19,750	3,188	9,148
Winning Trades	7,046	1,114	6,212
Losing Trades	12,474	2,055	5,806
Win %	36.096	35.153	35.618
Profit Factor (Profit on Winning Trades/Loss on Losing Trades)	$1.12	$1.07	$1.10
Total Profits	$48,069,000	$5,028,000	$76,069,000
Adding the Two Strategies Together as Separate Programs =			$53,097,000
Benefits of Dynamically Rebalancing tthe Strategies Together =			$22,972,000

Dynamically blending multiple strategies together generally will produce a better profit than running strategies by themselves with their own equity. Essentially what happens is that each strategy gets the benefit of more equity when they are struggling and end up getting less when other strategies in the portfolio are struggling. This smooths the profits from each strategy and allows the total portfolio to produce more profits.

The longer-term strategy didn't really have a great period to make very high returns but had a lot fewer trades. The percent reliability of these two models was below 50 percent as expected with typical trend-following models. Combining the two strategies improved a few return-to-risk ratios and reduced the overall drawdown while slightly increasing returns. The number of trades decreased because many times both strategies might be in the same market in opposite directions, negating the position. The simulation platform correctly would assume there was no trade.

I could run even more strategies together and get continued benefits to the statistics. That's why I currently run nine strategies using 40–70 positions in ETFs, futures, and options over four different time periods and multiple indicators. Each additional strategy incrementally makes for more work but keeps my mental side focused on running the strategies and not getting emotional over any one trade or strategy. I get better return to risks, lower drawdown potential, more consistency, and the ability to be serene.

9

FILLING THE "POTHOLES"

LAURENS BENSDORP, A FRIEND AND EXPERIENCED trader mentioned in the previous chapter, likens adding more strategies to the mix to "filling the potholes" in your equity curve. I love this analogy, because it is so easy to visualize what you are trying to do. Adding non-correlated strategies, additional markets, and additional time periods that are likely to produce a profit when your existing strategies are struggling will help fill the potholes. Below is a sample chart of some "filling the potholes" so that you have a visual of this concept.

The shaded areas are the times when traders will be most ill at ease and are likely to abandon their well-laid-out plans. Our goal in attempting to fill the "potholes" is to create strategies that are more likely to create potential for profit in those time periods and that type of market action.

GRAPHIC 30—FILLING THE "POTHOLES"

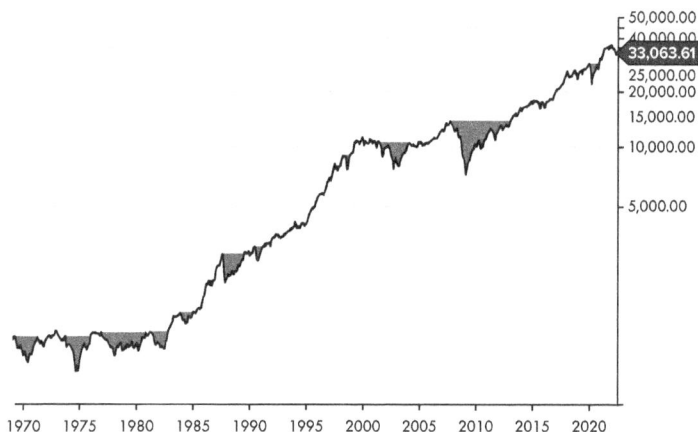

SOME SIMPLE EXAMPLES OF "FILLING THE POTHOLES"

Let's say you start out with a simple long-term, long only trend-following strategy on broadly based ETFs. You run some simulations and to nobody's surprise, the strategy seems to produce nice profits during up moves in the general stock market, remains in cash for long periods during major bear markets, and has significant drawdowns during transitions from up to down and during sideways periods.

What if we add a shorter-term long/short trend following on a stock index futures contract? Every time it goes short, the total portfolio is hedged, and potential for losses is minimized. In sideways periods the long and short trades might pick up some short-term profits to offset some of the drawdown in the very long-term strategy potential for costly whipsaws. What you've done is to understand when, where, and how one strategy will struggle and why another strategy can pick up some of the slack.

What if you concentrate on just tech stocks? When the NASDAQ, which includes a lot of these companies, goes into a slide, you will expect to lose money in the portfolio. Then how about adding a diversified portfolio of futures contracts that does not include any stock-related positions? Extreme diversification allows that new part of the portfolio to potentially produce profits to offset some of the weakness in your tech stock portfolio.

In another example, you have one strategy you run each day. You are an expert in selling option premiums in both directions of the stock market: Up and Down. Where are your risks here? Well, if you sell a call for its premium and the stock market takes off to the upside, you potentially have a seriously large loss potential. What might you do to create more All-Weather thinking in that case? Perhaps look at a longer-term strategy in similar positions, so that in runaway bull or bear markets, you are making a large profit in the trend following to offset the hit you are taking in selling options. Capturing option premiums should do very well during sideways periods, so the two strategies will be synergistic, helping to stabilize your overall results and creating an All-Weather effect.

An Example from My Own Portfolio

I took several of my own strategies that I have cobbled together over the years, and I'll spare you the details on each one, since some of them I've already mentioned. The name I've given each strategy should be enough to give you an idea of generally what that approach is trading and trying to focus on for its part of the total portfolio. I'll use $10 million for the starting equity on each run to make sure that capital isn't keeping out some of the strategies or positions along the way. This makes the simulations less dependent on equity and provides a better view of each strategy's potential. The list of strategies for this example is:

- Sector ETF Timing – thirty sector ETFs, long-term trend following

- ES Futures Hedging – Short-only hedge for long exposure from Sector ETF Timing

- Diversified Futures Timing – twenty-six markets, long-term trend following

- NQ Futures Timing – Long/Short positions using short-term trend-following models

- Futures Counter-Trend – Extremely short-term Long/Short trend following

- Crypto Futures Timing – Long/Short positions on BTC/ETH using short-term trend following

Sim Trader

GRAPHIC 31—SECTOR COMBINED WITH ES HEDGING

STRATEGY ALLOCATION LETTER	A	B	C
SIMULATION STATISTIC NAME	SECTOR ETF TIMING 100%	ES FUTURES HEDGING 100%	COMBINED STRATEGIES % 50/25
Average Compound Growth Rate %	+18.126	-0.627	+9.610
Sharpe Ratio	0.872	0.606	0.849
Sortino Ratio	1.150	0.884	1.116
MAR Ratio (Return/ Max Drawdown)	0.467	0.066	0.451
Average Drawdown %	-4.527	-2.765	-2.411
Maximum Drawdown %	-38.830	-9.573	-21.311
Maximum Time Spent in a Drawdown	885 days	4,376 days	884 days
Number of Total Trades in 12.4 Years	1,048	28	1,076
Number of Positive Trades in 12.4 Years	500	9	513
Number of Negative Trades in 12.4 Years	548	19	563
% Profitability	47.710	32.143	47.677
Profits on $10MM in 12.4 Years	$66,535,517	$731,263	$20,689,108
Profit Factor per Average Trade	$1.56	$0.42	$1.66

You can tell from the descriptions that there's a lot going on here. This requires some automation and a lot of organizing of the pieces of the puzzles, but here's the prize available if you can organize your own trading in more of an All-Weather collection of strategies in the tables on the next few pages. First up, let's base load the portfolio with my Sector ETF Timing Strategy and add in some ES Futures Hedging and see how it affects the performance statistics. Remember that when we combine strategies, we must reduce the commitment to each one, so that we do not run out of equity.

Looks like for the protection of the long side of sector timing, we paid a small price in profits, returns, and all the return-to-risk ratios declined. We also had to execute a few more trades. Note that I ran the combined case with only 50 percent of the equity dedicated to the Sector ETF Timing and only 25 percent of the equity allocated to the ES Hedging, and profits declined somewhat due to that deleveraging. Next let's use some extreme diversification and add in a longer-term trend-following futures portfolio of twenty-six liquid markets long and short. We will need to adjust the percent allocation to each of the strategies, so that we can spread the equity out over additional strategies. Results are shown in Graphic 32.

Notice that the combinations are improving some of the return-to-risk numbers, reducing drawdowns, improving the returns, and increasing the profits. The number of trades is continuing to climb as expected since we are adding additional markets and strategies.

Sim Trader

GRAPHIC 32—ADDING DIVERSIFIED FUTURES TIMING

STRATEGY ALLOCATION LETTER	C	D	E
SIMULATION STATISTIC NAME	COMBINED STRATEGIES % 50/25	DIVERSIFIED FUTURES TIMING 100%	COMBINED STRATEGIES % 50/25/50
Average Compound Growth Rate %	+9.610	+11.337	+15.551
Sharpe Ratio	0.849	0.861	1.162
Sortino Ratio	1.116	1.430	1.656
MAR Ratio (Return/ Max Drawdown)	0.451	0.588	0.804
Average Drawdown %	-2.411%	-4.343%	-3.074%
Maximum Drawdown %	-21.311%	-19.274%	-19.348%
Maximum Time Spent in a Drawdown	884 Days	884 Days	413 Days
Number of Total Trades in 12.4 Years	1,076	7,202	8,278
Number of Positive Trades in 12.4 Years	513	2,596	3,114
Number of Negative Trades in 12.4 Years	563	4,504	5,062
% Profitability	47.677	36.563	38.087
Profits on $10MM in 12.4 Years	$20,689,108	$26,956,176	$49,338,262
Profit Factor per Average Trade	$1.66	$1.11	$1.23

Sim Trader

GRAPHIC 33—ADDING SHORT-TERM NQ FUTURES TIMING

STRATEGY ALLOCATION LETTER	E	F	G
SIMULATION STATISTIC NAME	COMBINED STRATEGIES % 50/25/50	ST NQ INDEX TIMING 100%	COMBINED STRATEGIES % 50/25/50/25
Average Compound Growth Rate %	+15.551	+0.186	+15.693
Sharpe Ratio	1.162	0.023	1.162
Sortino Ratio	1.656	0.031	1.652
MAR Ratio (Return/ Max Drawdown)	0.804	0.008	0.799
Average Drawdown %	-3.074	-1.784	-3.132
Maximum Drawdown %	-19.348	-23.852	-19.642
Maximum Time Spent in a Drawdown	413 Days	3,689 Days	507 Days
Number of Total Trades in 12.4 Years	8,278	262	8,512
Number of Positive Trades in 12.4 Years	3,114	91	3,196
Number of Negative Trades in 12.4 Years	5,062	171	5,214
% Profitability	38.087	34.733	38.002
Profits on $10MM in 12.4 Years	$49,338,262	$232,685	$50,247,881
Profit Factor per Average Trade	$1.23	$1.03	$1.23

Let's add into the mix my Short-Term NQ Timing (9-Day) Program that helps juice upside returns when the markets are on the upside and helps provide a bit of an early hedge in down moves. This strategy is trying to pick up profits from shorter-term moves in the stock market. Results are shown in Graphic 33.

With this addition, the combined portfolio has made little progress in most of the metrics over the time period of this simulation. Still, with the addition of the extra strategy, we've given the overall portfolio more ability to deal with varied market conditions, so I would anticipate surviving and prospering in more types of markets. My judgment is to keep it in the mix to help fill future "potholes."

Next up let's add some very short-term three-day-oriented futures trading on the same portfolio that we used in Case D going back a couple of pages. Results are shown in Graphic 34.

Adding in the very short-term futures program helped the cause quite a bit. The numbers of the strategy by itself were decent, and the diversification it added to the other four strategies we've looked at so far was excellent. Every statistic was improved with higher returns, higher return-to-risk measurements, lower drawdowns, and less time spent in the maximum drawdown.

Now we'll add the last strategy. When cryptos came into being, I was slow to trade them directly, but the CME created futures on cryptos. Since I am very familiar with trading futures, that was an easier market to add to the overall portfolio. I used the same nine-day shorter-term trend-following approach for the

crypto futures that I used for NQ Timing and added it to the
mix. Results are shown in Graphic 35.

Sim Trader

GRAPHIC 34—ADDING SHORT-TERM FUTURES TIMING

STRATEGY ALLOCATION LETTER	G	H	I
SIMULATION STATISTIC NAME	COMBINED STRATEGIES % 50/25/50/25	ST 3-DAY FUTURES 100%	COMBINED STRATEGIES % 50/25/50/25/50
Average Compound Growth Rate %	+15.693	+15.121	+24.858
Sharpe Ratio	1.162	1.563	1.591
Sortino Ratio	1.652	2.360	2.408
MAR Ratio (Return/ Max Drawdown)	0.799	1.102	1.134
Average Drawdown %	-3.132	-1.732	-3.127
Maximum Drawdown %	-19.642	-13.723	-21.923
Maximum Time Spent in a Drawdown	507 Days	681 Days	490 Days
Number of Total Trades in 12.4 Years	8,512	19,750	11,702
Number of Positive Trades in 12.4 Years	3,196	7,046	4,351
Number of Negative Trades in 12.4 Years	5,214	12,474	7,218
% Profitability	38.002	36.096	37.609
Profits on $10MM in 12.4 Years	$50,247,881	$48,069,112	$145,766,893
Profit Factor per Average Trade	$1.23	$1.12	$1.17

Sim Trader

GRAPHIC 35—ADDING CRYPTO FUTURES TIMING

STRATEGY ALLOCATION LETTER	I	J	K
SIMULATION STATISTIC NAME	COMBINED STRATEGIES % 50/25/50/25/50	CRYPTO FUTURES SHORT TERM 100%	6 COMBINED STRATEGIES % 50/25/50/25/50/50
Average Compound Growth Rate %	+24.858	+0.712	+25.751
Sharpe Ratio	1.591	1.493	1.637
Sortino Ratio	2.408	2.328	2.482
MAR Ratio (Return/ Max Drawdown)	1.134	0.256	1.175
Average Drawdown %	-3.127	-0.720	-3.086
Maximum Drawdown %	-21.923	-2.785	-21.923
Maximum Time Spent in a Drawdown	490 Days	88 Days	490 Days
Number of Total Trades in 12.4 Years	11,702	14	11,717
Number of Positive Trades in 12.4 Years	4,351	8	4,357
Number of Negative Trades in 12.4 Years	7,218	6	7,226
% Profitability	37.609	57.143	37.615
Profits on $10MM in 12.4 Years	$145,766,893	$915,981	$160,172,252
Profit Factor per Average Trade	$1.17	$3.13	$1.18

We have arrived at a combination of six of the same strategies I use today in my own portfolio. Notice that we're using 250 percent of the equity in the account. We can do that because many of the futures strategies use only a fraction of the equity for margin. For every $100,000 of equity, I might be tying up a few thousand dollars of required margins. I'm overlaying security and futures together in one portfolio, creating efficiencies in the use of cash.

These strategies are subject to change when I get a good new idea, but I wanted to give you a sense of the progression in my thinking and how I decided to diversify the total portfolio by strategy, by market, and by time period. Every single statistic improved in the end over the starting base case of simple Sector ETF Timing. We had more return, better return-to-risk, smaller and less lengthy drawdowns, and more profits. The only thing that has been a negative in my retirement is having to do more trades to get there, but if I can have a combination of strategies, markets, and time periods that can get anywhere near the number in Case K, I'll do the extra work necessary. Look at where we started and where we ended up.

For those of you reading this book with a calculator, you may notice that if you add some cases together, they might not perfectly add up. The simulator I used dynamically rebalanced things like equity among the strategies every day of the simulation. A strategy that might be in a losing streak may buy into a larger position due to getting its normal share of dollars from profits coming from other strategies. Generally, you'll notice that if you arithmetically add the various strategies, it will not come anywhere near where the dynamically rebalanced portfolio finishes. By smoothing the track record, compounding the returns, and leveraging the cash being used, the dynamically rebalanced combination makes more progress on many fronts than any one strategy by itself.

A number of disclaimers are appropriate here. Theoretical simulations have to be taken with a grain of salt. The data is a finite part of history. The future for every market is changing all the time. More computers, more volume, wider market participants, instant communication, and more markets to trade mean the future will always be different. However, in my mind, if you have chosen a destination, you can figure out how to get there. Hopefully, I've provided a bit of a road map.

You are not going to get perfect fills on every trade. The simulation platform did properly consider gap openings, but many will go against you. Commissions, while being very small or nonexistent these days, may add a small burden to overcome in the real world.

I started every single simulation with a $10 million portfolio. I wanted to remove from the simulations any chance that I would have a portfolio size limitation to the strategies. With less equity and by limiting position size as a percent of equity, it is possible to have some trades drop out of the mix, giving you somewhat granular results, depending more on the size of the account than on the concepts I'm describing. Of course, almost everyone reading the book will not have $10 million, but if the concepts are sound, your results will simply be slightly off due to some of the trades dropping out of the mix with the smaller account size.

Sim Trader

GRAPHIC 36—STARTING POINT AND WHERE WE ARE NOW

STRATEGY ALLOCATION LETTER	A	K
SIMULATION STATISTIC NAME	STARTING SECTOR ETF TIMING	6 COMBINED STRATEGIES % 50/25/50/25/50/50
Average Compound Growth Rate %	+18.126	+25.751
Sharpe Ratio	0.872	1.637
Sortino Ratio	1.150	2.482
MAR Ratio (Return/Max Drawdown)	0.467	1.175
Average Drawdown %	-4.527	-3.086
Maximum Drawdown %	-38.830	-21.923
Maximum Time Spent in a Drawdown	885 Days	490 Days
Number of Total Trades in 12.4 Years	1,048	11,717
Number of Positive Trades in 12.4 Years	500	4,357
Number of Negative Trades in 12.4 Years	548	7,226
Percent Profitability %	47.710	37.615
Profits on $10MM in 12.4 Years	$66,535,517	$160,172,252
Profit Factor Per Average Trade	$1.56	$1.18

The trading volume of some 11,717 trades over the simulation may seem daunting to some, but it works out to 944 trades per year on average and, in a 250-day trading year, about 3.78 trades per day. If you have the time or the automation for some or all of that, it's not that intimidating. I do it every day, and it gets fairly boring and mechanical after a while.

What are you currently doing with your portfolio? What types of market action will likely create risk and poor performance? What type of strategy and set of indicators or time periods would likely create a benefit during the same periods when your original portfolio should be struggling? Getting into that mindset and answering these questions will help you "fill the potholes" and become an All-Weather Trader.

10

HOW MUCH
DO WE BUY OR SELL?

POSITION SIZING IS MORE IMPORTANT THAN YOUR BUY/
Sell engine. But why does almost every trader starting out their
journey in trading spend most of his time browsing through
ways to buy and sell? Your trading profit on any trade is the
price at which you sell minus the price at which you buy *times
the size of your position*. It does not make any sense to concern
yourself with the first part of the formula and ignore the second
part. Yet so many traders spend little time thinking though the
sizing of their trades.

I wrote a book on the subject, *Successful Traders Size Their
Positions—Why and How?* You can find it any number of places
including my website enjoytheride.world, and this chapter
contains some of my key points.

The first thing that comes to mind is the extreme importance of sizing your portfolio. Put less effort into analyzing charts, indicators, and books trying to find the best triggers to buy or sell trading instruments. Put more effort into optimizing and understanding position sizing.

When you analyze the impact of the Buy/Sell engine, you realize that jumping on a huge move or trend at one point using one indicator, versus a few hours later using another indicator, means very little to your profits should a large move happen in your direction. It might end up being a 60 percent profit versus a 59.8 percent profit on the trade. Spending a lot of time researching the key to getting the 60 percent trade becomes an exercise with diminishing returns on your effort. The important thing is to get on the trend somewhere, so that you are positioned with momentum.

How much to buy or sell has a lot more impact on your long-term success. Take on too much of the position and you increase the chances of wrecking your portfolio long-term. Take on too little, and you are not going to create enough return on a good trade to pay you for the effort. So how can we find a personal sweet spot where the positions are properly sized?

EQUITY DRIVES THE SIZE OF YOUR POSITIONS

It seems logical to me that everything in position sizing should start with the equity in your account. Simply put, if you have a larger portfolio, you'll need larger position sizes to have the optimal effect. Smaller portfolios need smaller positions.

What drives emotional reactions to market action by traders? I maintain that the risk of losing money and volatility are the two most likely culprits. The risk of a trade brings the fear of losing real dollars if you are wrong. Volatility of the position up and down in any period can also grab your attention and create some angst.

Put simply, we want to size our positions so that the risk is reasonable by our own standards, and the volatility of the position doesn't keep us up at night. Starting with the risk of the trade and a current measure of volatility, it becomes easy to set a level where each trader is comfortable and limit the initial size of the position to that level.

One important point is that many traders control risk by first deciding on their position size and entry and then moving their stop loss point up or down to create a potential risk where they can tolerate the loss.

This is backward!

The market doesn't care that you can only tolerate a 5 or 10 percent loss. The market does what the market does. If the market is extremely quiet, maybe placing a 4 or 5 percent stop loss order makes sense. However, if the market is moving up and down 2to 3 percent per day and the news is all over the place, placing a stop order too close to the action will just get you stopped out, and you may miss out on a good trade.

By creating a Buy/Sell strategy that allows sufficient room for the market to make "normal" movement and measuring the risk and volatility on one unit of that instrument, you can size your position appropriately no matter what the market's conditions are. The crazier the market is, the smaller your positions automatically become. And, when markets are quiet and "normal," you automatically get larger positions.

A Simple Example of Sizing Your Initial Position

Let's create a simple example of a stock (XYZ) being purchased for a $100,000 portfolio. Normal movement up and down has XYZ currently in a sideways market. The top of the range is $10, and the bottom is $9. We could say that above $10, we are in an Uptrend and below $9 we are in a Downtrend. Between $10 and $9, we are in noise, which we ignore. Let's buy it on the Uptrend at $10.01 and put in a stop loss order at $8.99. Volatility as measured by the Average True Range over the last twenty-one days is currently running $0.50.

We would have already determined a number of limits that we are comfortable with in sizing all new positions in the portfolio. We decided that with our portfolio, we'd rather not have a position larger than 10 percent of the portfolio and that the risk from any one new position should not be any more than 1 percent of our equity. We also decided that the volatility of the new position should not move our equity more than 0.5 percent in a single day. So, let's see how easily we size the position.

Risk Method:

$100,000 * 1% = $1,000 allowed risk / ($10.01 - $8.99) = 980.39 shares

Rounded down to the nearest whole share = **980 shares**

Volatility Method:

$100,000 * 0.5% = $500 allowed volatility / $0.50 = **1,000 shares**

Percent of Portfolio Method:

$100,000 * 10% = $10,000 maximum in the position / $10.01 price = **999 shares**

Since I am looking for a position size that doesn't grab my attention, I always opt for the smallest position size calculated. In this example that would be the Risk Method or **980 shares** of XYZ.

An Example of Sizing a Futures Trade

The same process can be applied to a futures position. Let's keep it simple with the same $100,000 portfolio. The range on MES March contracts (S&P 500 micro futures) has been from 4,959 to 4,901, and the Average True Range volatility average over the last twenty-one days is running twenty points per day. We don't want our risk on the position to exceed 1 percent of our equity,

and we don't want the MES futures contract pushing our portfolio around more than 0.5 percent per day due to volatility.

Our indicators are telling us that MES is now breaking out
lower at 4,900; our stop is above the range at 4,960, giving us
sixty points of risk on this trade. Each point of risk on one ES
contract is worth $5. The required margin to sell one MES
contract is $1,600. So, let's see how to calculate our size for this
MES trade.

Risk Method:

$100,000 * 1% = $1,000 allowed risk / ((4960 - 4900) * $5) =
$1,000 / $300 = 3.33 contracts

Rounded down to the nearest contract would be **3 contracts**

Volatility Method:

$100,000 * 0.5% = $500 allowed volatility / (20 Points * $5) =
$500/ $100 = **5 contracts**

Percent of Portfolio Method:

$100,000 * 10% = $10,000 maximum in the position

Margin required for one MES Contract = $1,600 so $10,000 /
$1,600 = **6.25 contracts**

Rounded down = **6 contracts**

I look for the smallest position calculated to maximize my comfort level, so it looks like the risk method is the winner here with **3 contracts**, and that's how many I would sell on the breakout.

YOUR SIZING JOB DOES NOT END HERE

Now you are into the trade. Conditions are changing every day. Let say you've been in the trade for three weeks and things have gotten a lot more exciting. Some piece of news (e.g., pandemic, war, OPEC decisions, political turmoil) has caused the position you are trading to go wild. Even though you properly sized your initial position, your work doesn't end there. The market has changed, so you have to stay on top of it and make sure you maintain a properly sized position.

Over the decades that I have traded, I have noticed that frequently quiet, uninteresting markets start a move with nobody caring. As the trend continues, more traders get into the trend, and it starts becoming interesting. It might make the evening news or the financial newspapers and blogs. Risk becomes greater, as does volatility, in that scenario. Maybe you've allowed the trend to mature, and you are now profitable. So, how can we maintain a reasonable exposure on the ongoing trade?

Ongoing Trade in Stocks

Let's continue the simple example of stock XYZ. Our hypothetical portfolio has grown to $120,000. Normal movement has

XYZ in an Up market. The stock is now $15, and the stop has moved up to $10.75 according to our Buy/Sell engine. The risk is $4.25, much higher than it was when we got into the stock. Volatility has increased to $1.25 over the last twenty-one days as measured by ATR.

We have to allow more for risk and volatility in an existing position. We want our position to increase in risk a little, since we are in a winning position and can afford to give it a bit more of the risk allocation in the portfolio, allowing it to continue to trend in our direction. Let's say that we can tolerate an existing winner to have 2.5 percent risk. We still do not want anything to be more than 10 percent of our portfolio. We also decided that the volatility of the new position should not move our equity more than 0.7 percent in a single day. Let's see how we size the ongoing position.

Risk Method:

$120,000 * 2.5% = $3,000 allowed risk / ($4.25 risk) = 705.88 shares

Rounded down to the nearest whole share = **705 shares**

Volatility Method:

$120,000 * 0.7% = $840 allowed volatility / $1.25 = **672 shares**

Percent of Portfolio Method:

$120,000 * 10% = $12,000 maximum in the position / $15.00 price = **800 shares**

Continuing with the philosophy that I want the most conservative exposure that gets the job done, I'll take the Volatility Method's **672 shares** for my XYZ position. That means selling off 980 – 672 shares, or 308 shares, at market.

Ongoing Sizing in Futures

The ongoing sizing control will be similar to what we just covered in the stock position sizing. Let's use the same increased $120,000 portfolio. The price move on MES March contracts (S&P 500 micro futures) has been lower and profitable. It has fallen to 4750 while the stop has moved down to 4875 for a risk of 125 points. The ATR volatility average over the last twenty-one days is now at 100 points per day, twice what it was when we got into the sell. We don't want our risk of the position to exceed 2.5 percent of our equity, and we don't want the MES futures contract pushing our portfolio around more than 0.7 percent per day.

Since margin is set any particular day by the exchanges and the broker you're dealing with, let's say due to the exciting times in the MES market, margin has been increased to $2,000 for every contract you own. Let's look at how to calculate our ongoing size at this point for this MES trade.

Risk Method:

$120,000 * 2.5% = $3,000 allowed risk / (125 points risk * $5) = $3,000 / $625 = **4.8 contracts**

Rounded down to the nearest contract = **4 contracts**

Volatility Method:

$120,000 * 0.7% = $840 allowed volatility / (100 Pts (ATR) * $5) = $840/ $500 = **1.68 contracts**

Rounded down = **1 contract**

Percent of Portfolio Method:

$120,000 * 10% = $12,000 maximum in the position

Margin required for one MES contract = $2,000 so $12,000 / $2,000 = **6 contracts**

Once again, I err on the conservative side of things and would take the smallest answer, which would be Volatility Method at **1 contract**. I started with a position size of 3, so I'd sell off 2 contracts at market to bring my allocation into my comfort level for ongoing, profitable trades.

MANAGING TOTAL PORTFOLIO RISK AND VOLATILITY

Now that you understand how you might control the sizes of stock and futures positions, we can move on to the subject of overall portfolio risk and volatility. For instance, if we had ten stocks in a portfolio, each of which has an average volatility of 0.5 percent per day, we might see 10 times 0.5 or 5 percent, swings in our portfolio on a normal day. That might be hard for some traders to take. Controlling your portfolio's overall risk and volatility is one more way to smooth out the ride.

Let's say you can only tolerate a 5 percent overall volatility in the portfolio, and you don't want your total risk in the portfolio to exceed 14 percent on a given day. Simply add up the positions and see if you are over those predetermined levels. If you are, just "peel off" enough of each position to bring you back down to your comfort level.

Now I know that some sharp statistician will now be saying, "Yeah, but what about the lack of correlations between the positions? You can't simply add the risk and volatility numbers. Some might be volatile up and others volatile down in the same day, offsetting each other." As far as I'm concerned, keeping it simple and conservative outweighs complex calculations. Taking correlations into account might allow you to hold more positions and larger position sizes but involves a lot more calculations and still might not be precisely correct due to constantly changing correlations.

In addition, if you had watched correlation among various positions in the portfolio for multiple decades as I have, you'd have seen times when a world crisis, panic bear market, or other news shoves all the correlations to near 1.00 or very correlated. Why not keep it simple, assume that all the positions are 100 percent correlated, and make your All-Weather Trader's life a bit easier?

If I need to "peel off" 2 percent to bring the total portfolio risk or volatility down to acceptable levels, I just multiply 2 percent by each position's existing size, round it to a whole unit (share or contract), and liquidate that immediately at market. The portfolio will have lower overall risk, less volatility, and a smoother equity curve. In addition, studies that I have done going back to my money management career show that this concept will improve your return-to-risk ratios. It is essentially reducing the size of the potential next drawdown, which is coming at you from right around the corner.

SUMMARY OF THE BENEFITS OF ADDING VARIOUS LEVELS OF SIZING

I thought it might be useful for traders to see the incremental benefits of going through each level of position sizing using a single simple trend-following strategy. The following table shows the case I ran in the simulation platform on a twenty-six-market futures portfolio using some standard trend-following indicators and the salient statistics on each simulation. The same indicators and portfolio were fixed in this table. The only change was the position-sizing algorithms "managing" the position size. You can see that adding in position-sizing concepts to your portfolio yields some benefits to the All-Weather portfolio.

Sim Trader

GRAPHIC 37—INCREMENTAL BENEFITS OF POSITION SIZING—ADD EACH LAYER SEQUENTIALLY

PARAMETER	PARAMETER VALUE	ACGR %	SORTINO RATIO	MAX DRAW-DOWN %	RETURN/MAX DRAWDOWN
Initial Risk % of Equity	0.5	+15.087	0.876	-87.142	0.173
Ongoing Risk % of Equity	1.0	+13.797	0.844	-63.864	0.216
Initial Vol % of Equity	0.2	+11.223	1.409	-19.507	0.575
Ongoing Vol % of Equity	0.5	+11.377	1.426	-19.255	0.591
Total Risk Portfolio %	15.0	+11.343	1.436	-19.266	0.589
Total Vol Portfolio %	7.0	+11.343	1.436	-19.266	0.589

The progression of the results against adding each additional position-sizing parameter shows a logical improvement in the stats. Starting with a simplistic 0.5 percent risk to equity level, we see that the ride can indeed be wild. Most traders couldn't stick around for that kind of pain. Add some ongoing risk control, set at 1.0 percent and we see an expected slight drop in returns, but improvements in return-to-risk rations and drawdown percent. Add in volatility control of the initial position and the return drops some more, but we've now more than doubled the Sortino ratio, dramatically cut the drawdown, and jumped the return to maximum drawdown 3.3 times the original case. Add in ongoing volatility controls set to 0.4 percent and we actually improve return slightly, but also improve all the rest of the stats. Finally add in portfolio-level risk and volatility controls, and the returns, maximum drawdown, and the return to maximum drawdown remain steady. The Sortino ratio keeps getting better, ending at its highest level of all the cases. You are now reaching the point of diminishing returns on any more fine-tuning of the position controls.

The lesson I see in these runs is that controlling position sizes over literally thousands of trades in these simulations improves the behavior of the strategy. All these runs were with the same exact basic futures strategy I use now as I write this book. I'm striving for decent returns for my retirement portfolio, drawdowns that I can tolerate, and decent return-to-risk measure. Position sizing helps get me there. This is just one strategy. Imagine how this helps if you do it across multiple markets, strategies, and time periods. Take the time to explore this in your portfolio. It has always helped my consistency comfort levels in trading.

DIALING IN YOUR OWN ALL-WEATHER POSITION SIZING

I chose the numbers I did for all the examples because they're easy to work with; each trader has his own risk and volatility tolerance levels and should customize sizing controls for his situation. If you are a new trader and aren't sure what your pain tolerance is, start low and work your way up. Do not start high and work your way down. That would be a recipe for disaster.

If you believe that you could tolerate 1 percent risk on a new position, maybe start well below that at 0.5 or 0.6 percent, try it for a while, and increase it if it seems a bit too tame for you. Always err on the low side. Long-term, with the market throwing record levels of risk and volatility at you, you will appreciate trading with position-sizing controls in place that match your situation and psyche. This will help you keep on trading your strategy where poor position sizing might have caused you to abandon managing your portfolio out of frustration or anxiety.

11

THE MENTAL SIDE
OF TRADING

WHY SHOULD WE CARE ABOUT THE
MENTAL ASPECTS OF TRADING?

Dr. Van K. Tharp always said, "Traders don't trade the markets; they trade their beliefs." I agree completely. Everything I have described in this book explains my beliefs. Here they are:

1. A successful trader has a Buy/Sell engine that makes sense and helps him pull the trigger.

2. A successful trader has a sensible approach to systematically sizing his positions, helping to reduce the probability of ruin.

3. A successful trader has strategies that help fill the drawdown "potholes" in the equity curves to makes it all less stressful.

4. Markets go up, down, and sideways over time.

5. Creating an overall strategy or collection of strategies that matches your situation well is a much more successful approach to trading than copying someone else's hot strategy that you will unlikely be able to execute over time.

6. Nothing is perfect in trading.

7. The market will do what the market will do.

I still remember hearing Dr. Tharp in one of his Peak Performance seminars ask the group what is more important: the Buy/Sell, the sizing of your position, or your mental trading acumen? Some guessed that without the ability to trigger the buy or sell, there is no trade. Others would say, "Yes, but if you don't size the position correctly, the trade could go against you, and you might be knocked out of the game." These are both valid points, but the most important aspect of trading is your mental process. Without it, nothing else good happens.

At this point, and with my engineering background and reputation with computerizing things, I get the argument "But you're a systematic computer-driven trader. Your mental side of trading isn't as important as someone who sits there all day in front of the computer." That is, of course, not true. I'm the guy who has to hit the button to run those programs. I can skip it today if I want. I can set up the programs to give me alerts, then override the signals. I can feel strongly about a new trade and double the size that the computer had me buying. I can read something compelling and decide to "take a flyer" on some position that I've never traded before. There are infinite ways I could get in the way of the process. I'm human. My feelings can easily create mistakes, so I have to spend time getting the mental side of trading right.

This chapter is focused on building a foundation for a great **trading psyche.** I will use this term to describe your entire collection of mental processes that might affect your ability to be a successful All-Weather Trader. I like to think of each subsection below as a piece of what I call the trading psyche. They are all important to the process of success in trading.

SELF-ESTEEM

We'll start our mental journey here to lay a solid foundation. Self-esteem is how a person thinks and feels about his own qualities and characteristics.

In trading, as in most every endeavor, we want high self-esteem. The markets we trade have this insidious way of pushing our mental buttons and making us doubt ourselves. Having positive thoughts about your own qualities and characteristics helps counter the negative effects that the markets tend to throw at you over time.

Imagine the opposite. You put on a trade. It lasts one day, hits your stop loss order, and you are out. You took a loss. *You were wrong again.* You acted impulsively and didn't quite follow your strategy, and this is the third time in a row that you've screwed up something in your trading. You have a low opinion of yourself, and this trade and many others before it are just confirming that you are not good enough to do this.

Geez. I started getting depressed just writing that paragraph.

A better way to handle these potential stressors to your psyche is to first do whatever you can to realize that you have qualities and characteristics that nobody else has. You must believe you have special skills. You have a unique place in the world as a spouse, parent, child, friend, coworker, and part of your community. You have value. Do not define yourself as a trader. Define yourself as a person important to the world you live in. Have a high opinion of who you are. Really believe it because it is true! Nobody should have a low opinion of himself, but some still do. If this describes you, before starting your journey down the path of trading, work on valuing yourself more. This will have the added benefit of better overall health and well-being throughout your entire life, not just in trading.

RESPONSIBILITY

Next stop on our mental journey will be responsibility. As a child, I felt the world around me was this amazing place with so many exciting possibilities. Inside school, everything was scheduled. Outside of school delivering papers, reading books, and studying pretty much filled my days. As children, we all start out with parents and teachers controlling much of our world. We have very little responsibility for anything.

As we grow older, most of us realize that we are able to change things if we take responsibility for things that happen around us. Yet many fail to take on that responsibility. It is easy to blame someone or something else for things that happen, particularly negative events. Sometimes we like to take credit for positive events where we really just got lucky and had little to do with making them happen. "It's not my fault" becomes a cry for many. It is easy to play the victim. In trading it's "They ran my stops" or "My spouse interrupted me" or "The company manipulated the price of the stock with that announcement. Insiders must be selling out."

Responsibility gives you the ability to control so many things around you. If you decide that interruptions are causing a loss of focus, then you are responsible for creating an office situation that prevents distractions. If you have many stops getting executed too often and then reversing direction, take responsibility for measuring the noise, and see if you can figure out a way to give the market more room for it. If the news seems to cause you to act foolishly with your trading, turn off news.

Without self -responsibility, it's hard to be successful in anything. Without it the world will just keep on spinning and hitting you with random occurrences over and over again, and your life will be like a rowboat on the ocean in a storm, getting battered up, down, sideways, and ultimately capsizing. With responsibility, each person can assess the world around him and act to improve his situation or move toward achieving his goals. If you don't know anything about computer programming and decide that you would like to automate some of your trading processes, then you take responsibility to learn to code and build it. Or you might hire a computer science graduate and work with them to create programs to make your trading more effective and efficient.

If you set a stop, then fail to execute it, is it the market's fault or your own for failing to execute the stop? If you hire a programmer who creates a trading platform that simulates huge profits with some set of indicators, then quickly decide to start trading it real time and it blows up on you, was it the programmer's fault or yours for not checking and double-checking the results from the simulation and making sure the logic is working the way you need it to work?

If you get into a trade and the market moves against you, don't blame the market. The market can be fickle. As traders, we observe and react to it. The market doesn't care if we are trading or not. It does its thing. We take responsibility for reacting in a logical way to the way price moves play out.

Next time you find yourself placing blame elsewhere, instead ask yourself, "What could I have done or what could I do in the future that would result in a more positive outcome?" When you give yourself that power, it's amazing what you can accomplish.

AWARENESS

We'll start this subsection on trading psyche with a story of my own journey into the world of awareness. I've told this story countless times to help others start their own journeys into increased awareness.

When I was a senior in high school, I had to get up in front of an English class and give a report on a book I had just read for an assignment. I got up there, my hands shaking, and got through it somehow. Later that night, I sort of replayed the recording in my mind of what had gone on. I saw the faces of the friends I had known most of my life, watched my hands shaking, felt the fear I had when I got up in front of a group to speak, and realized that it was all illogical. My performance of a simple task in front of my friends was ridiculous. It made me mad that the event was the most significant of my day.

That review was so helpful that I started reviewing interactions and events of my day each night. I let whatever important event that had occurred pop into my head. I assumed that the few that came to mind were the most significant things that happened that day. I asked myself, "Is this the way I should behave or act in that situation? Was I happy with what happened? Is there anything I might have done differently?"

All this "reviewing the recording" helped guide me to improve my awareness and adjust the way I handled things. But I was a long way from being fully aware.

Fast-forward to playing basketball on a championship team as the center. From where I usually played on defense, I could see the rest my five-man team and most of the five guys we were playing against. So, I took it upon myself to call out what was happening behind some of my guys, since they did not have eyes in the back of their heads. This allowed them to concentrate on the opponent in front of them without taking their eyes off their opponent. It made our defense tougher. Most teams hated playing us because we would just shut down their ability to score.

Awareness came into play in basketball games in how I kept track of who was behind me. I was telling my teammates who was behind them, but there was nobody keeping track of who was behind me. I had to be aware of someone leaving my field of vision. If he came out the other side, that meant he was still behind me. I could then make sure that if a play looked like it would be coming my way, I was ready to make a move without even looking to see where the guy was. That helped train my mind to be aware of some things (guy behind me) while consciously processing other things (yelling out defensive instructions to my teammates).

I endured another test of awareness in a public speaking class at my chemical engineering job after college. I signed up for it right away, remembering my miserable performance in high school. The woman teaching the classes was excellent and had us all condensing our five- or ten-minute talks down to maybe three or four keywords listed on a small card. No written speech was needed. We had to simply take the first keyword and talk to the group. It was just like carrying on a regular conversation.

I rehearsed delivering my talks in front of a mirror. I'd be delivering the talk while watching myself deliver the talk. There were two things going on inside my brain, with one part actually speaking and the other part watching me speak. I noticed whether I was smiling or frowning or nervous or stumbling with my words. I practiced and performed better with increased awareness.

The other feedback loop that was set up was video recording. The teacher would videotape the talk each student gave and later in the class, play back the recording and suggest ways to improve our individual performances. We were all in the same boat, trying to get better, and it became a lot of fun for everyone. Laughing and giggling ensued, and we all kept getting better at talking in front of a group.

It was a little later, after I went into the money management business, that I knew I had to be aware of what was happening to me in real time, so I could guard against stress and rash actions that would cost my clients money. I thought of it as having an "Observer Self" on my shoulder taking in all that was happening in my life, not just speaking in front of a group. I actually put a sticky note on my computer screen that simply read "Awareness."

Whenever I saw the note, I would pause briefly to ask myself, "Was I aware?" If I was, great. If I wasn't, why not? I got better and better at being aware of what I was doing in real time. So, in contrast to my playing the tape back at the end of the day in high school, I was getting real-time awareness and the ability to adjust as I was going through life. Little by little, the Observer

Self simply merged into my mind, and I can now be aware of what is going on with myself all the time.

How does this relate to trading? If someone gives you a hot tip on a stock, and you are unaware of your greed, you cannot stop yourself from abandoning your trading strategy. If a position is caving in fast, approaching your stop loss, and you are getting stressed about it, being aware of your fear or nervousness allows you to pull back from negative mental states and remind yourself that the stop is there for a purpose and that the markets are unpredictable.

Without awareness, so many possibilities are eliminated. Everyone would be well served by acting out something in front of a mirror or video camera. Looking at yourself doing anything can provide you a useful skill in life and trading.

DISCIPLINE

I hear traders all the time talking about discipline in their trading. They override their strategy on a trade, then kick themselves for not being more disciplined. Traders will look at closing out a trade with a nice profit, only to see the trade continue on a tear and then say, "I wish I had the discipline to stay with my trades and let them run to larger profits."

This happens elsewhere in life as well. The person on a diet sees the piece of delicious chocolate cake and regrets eating it the next day. Someone decides to skip working out and then wonders why he feels sluggish the next couple of days. The person who usually goes to sleep at a reasonable time decides to read up on late-breaking news and has a hard time getting a good night's sleep.

So far, we've covered self-esteem, responsibility, and awareness, and all of them are essential to discipline. Lack of discipline can be doing something not in your plan. If you have great self-esteem, self-awareness, and self-responsibility, you will realize that you can be disciplined and take corrective action when you start to veer from your plan. Every time you do that and pat yourself on the back for your actions, you reinforce all the things you are doing mentally to make it easier to follow the disciplined choice in the future.

BALANCING YOUR MENTAL STATE

Our final stop on the journey through the mental side of trading is understanding, changing, and balancing mental states. Most traders, especially those with little awareness of what's happening to them, don't realize that their mental states may vary greatly from day to day. They also don't realize that mental states can help or hurt their trading. In addition, they don't even understand their own human ability to change their mental state to something more useful.

Let's look at some examples of mental states and how impactful they are to the trading process. In the first example, a trader gets news of the death of a loved one. He is in an extremely sad mental state. He is definitely not focused on the task at hand. Sadness doesn't give a trader an optimistic mental state needed to sustain a losing trade and keep on trading. He is much more likely in that mental state to say something like, "Screw this. I'm closing it down for the day."

Another trader just got news of an inheritance coming in, making his account flush with a lot of new money ready to be invested. He's feeling good, almost giddy. He's been on a tear with trading lately, producing some nice profits. In that mental state, he could easily take on more risk than would be normal or prudent. He might ignore risk and volatility-sizing suggestions and just "round the purchase up." He might easily overlook possible problems with the trade such as liquidity or the fact that the general market has been overbought for a while. Maybe it would be prudent to just continue to run his well-thought-out strategy instead.

In both these cases, one on the negative side and the other on the positive side, the traders were not in balanced mental states. Either of these extreme conditions can blind a trader to something that he should consider on the other side of the mental spectrum. The awareness that we talked about earlier is key here for realizing that you are now in an extreme mental state that is potentially hurtful to your trading.

So, let's say you realize that you're down or up, extremely angry or feeling silly. What can you do to change your mental state to one of balance? Being aware of your condition is the first step, but now you have to change to something more useful.

I like to watch the "movie of trading" or the "movie of life." Imagine right now that you are in a movie of your life. You are in every scene. Look around the room and see the people, your pets, perhaps the television, the trees outside swaying in the breeze. Do not focus on anything specific. When you watch a movie, you are being entertained or thrilled or scared or whatever else the film is trying to pull emotionally from the viewer. But you, of course, realize that it's just a movie. It's not real. You can keep coming back to that mental thought to keep you balanced watching the movie.

You can also do that same thing during your day. Practice disassociating yourself from what is happening around you. Watch the movie of life. "Oh, another loss?" That is totally expected. "Look at that: XYZ set up another trade to go long." Time to get the trade on. No emotion. No stress or strain. You are just watching the movie and you are in every scene of the movie playing your part perfectly.

Just like movies frequently throw plot twists at you and surprise you, life includes some unexpected things. You can easily get sucked up into the surprises, and they can pull you off your beautifully balanced mental state. Think of the surprises as plot twists in your movie, and your character deals with the surprise with great efficiency and keeps focused on what he needs to do.

You can choose to become attached to an emotional state of mind or not. If you wanted to watch a comedy and decided you wanted a good laugh, you can let yourself be humored by the movie. If you wanted to be completely detached and watch the movie analyzing the sets, costumes, and characters, you might not find it all that amusing. If a football team goes into a game believing that they are going to lose, they will have an easy time making that a reality. If they instead concentrate on playing their positions and think, "We'll see what happens," they have a much better chance of playing their best.

It's totally within your power as a human to decide whether or not you wish to remain in an emotional mental state or not. If you realize that you are in a non-helpful mental state, change it to something that is helpful, and enjoy watching the movie of your life.

12

GETTING STARTED WITH ALL-WEATHER INVESTING

WHY DISCUSS THE ADVANTAGES AND MENTAL ASPECTS of trading with an All-Weather approach before getting into the details of how to implement it? You need a foundation, and you have slowly been building it. Now as you pursue your plan, you will be aware of what's to come. You know for the most part what to expect. And you can deal with those challenges accordingly.

It's time to begin your process. It's time to investigate which markets will work best for you—to study—to implement. It's an exciting time once you find a process and a set of markets that fit well with your personality. This allows you to become more optimistic about the outcome of your portfolio.

I am running an extremely diversified multiple-strategy All-Weather approach for our retirement accounts. I was not born with a knowledge of how to trade, how to size my positions, how to program computers, or how to change my mental states. I had to learn these things. I needed something I did not have and had to work to acquire it. Day after day, knowing where I was headed, I observed, learned from my mistakes, took courses, read books, and simulated trading strategies that made sense to me to manage the overall portfolio better than I had in the past.

This progression, however, isn't one that can occur overnight. If the goal is to take on this All-Weather Investing approach yourself, you will want to do the necessary work before diving in.

IMPLEMENTING AN ALL-WEATHER APPROACH

I like to break your work down into easily understandable steps. I recommend that you consider taking this implementation in the order I have listed as each step builds on the steps before it. Here's your working list:

1. *Take a personal inventory.* Write up a description of your future trading business as if you were going to present a business plan for a new venture. It should include things like capital, skills, people involved, time you will spend getting the business off the ground, and how much time you will spend each period executing the business. It will be unique to you, unlike any other trader out there.

2. *Decide on what markets you will trade.* Are you stock-oriented or futures-oriented or are you okay with trading anything if you can make it profitable?

What market do you already have a working knowledge of, and which would you like to diversify into that might require some learning?

3. *Create a Buy/Sell engine that will drive your trades.* It could be long term or short term. It might be a standard indicator. (Investopedia.com has dozens of them with formulas and logic.) It might use a computer or glance at a chart on your screen. Tailor it to you. Make sure you completely understand the logic and math involved. Try to ask yourself, "When will this type of indicator have its best performance and where will it likely struggle?" *Will that work for your needs?*

4. *Decide on a time period parameter.* A trader has to be able to pull information from what looks like noise or random data. A shorter-term period will tend to give you more trades, more things to do quickly and efficiently. Perhaps you are looking for challenges and want to day trade. Others may travel for their occupation and can look at the portfolio and indicators only once per week with reliability. Longer-term indicators would be helpful there. There is a time period that will fit your situation. *Find it, and put it into play.*

5. *Figure out how you will size the positions in your portfolio.* We covered some examples of how I approach that problem in Chapter 10. Perhaps you'd like to keep it simpler than I do, but have a logical plan to size the positions, so that every position in the portfolio can

contribute reward and risk to the entire effort. You do not want a single instrument dominating what is happening.

6. *Simulate what your strategy has done in the past to the extent you feel the need to.* If you are able to automate it, you might simply set up a simulation with time parameters that should work for you, a position-sizing concept that you like, and see what it looks like in history. Otherwise, you might go back on to your broker platform, look at some charts that occurred in Up, Down, and Sideways markets, and manually look at what happened to your strategy during those different periods. *The goal in this step is to understand more about how your strategy tends to perform in various market conditions.* You are getting more comfortable with what you will be running as an All-Weather Trader.

7. *Decide on a broker.* If you are going to trade just stocks, then you have numerous stock-only houses that can handle your trades. Some will allow for more automation, some less. If you want to be able to cover stock, option, and futures positions in your portfolio, you will have to seek out firms that are registered and operate in all those trading arenas. Having the ability to trade all your desired markets helps create efficiencies with your trading capital and a lot less hassle with moving money from broker to broker to rebalance your strategy.

8. *Get everything in place.* If you need a spreadsheet to size your positions, get it ready to go, and test it. Practice using it. Some broker platforms have a testing capability. Practice running your strategy each period for a while, actually inputting trades, checking your portfolio, rebalancing your portfolio if you need to, etc. This is like the military training for the next battle. They want to be prepared because their lives and those of their comrades depend on their performing well. Take the same attitude.

9. *Pull the trigger.* You've got your ducks in a row. You've prepared for the day. Your business is going to open its doors. No doubts now. As Larry the Cable Guy says, "Git-R-Done!"

Here are a few examples of how an implementation of an All-Weather approach might go:

Tim is a young career-minded individual with a computer background. He wants to be aggressive but is settling down and starting a family and doesn't want to go crazy with risk. Tim is fairly swamped at times at work, but wants to be hands-on with his investing, so he can learn and improve what he does over time.

So far, Tim has used a trading platform that his stock brokerage firm offered to execute stock trades in companies that interest him for the longer term. After many years of upside stock market, Tim's portfolio has grown nicely.

However, Tim knows from looking at historical charts that there's risk out there in the stock market. As we pointed out early in the book, stocks have taken some significant tumbles over the last dozen decades, and there's no reason to think they won't do the same in the future from time to time. Knowing this, Tim wants to find a way to be aggressive, yet manage the risk of potential future down stock markets.

Having access to his broker's trading platform and exploring it a bit, Tim noticed option information on stock indices was available and started exploring options as a potential hedge vehicle for his stock portfolio. Since his portfolio was largely aggressive positions in technology stocks, he decided to look at the options on the QQQ (Nasdaq 100) exchange traded fund. After talking to his broker and getting permission to trade options in his account, he decided to take a free beginner's course on options that he discovered on the internet. After understanding calls and puts, Tim decided to create a simple trend indicator on the platform to measure the stock market's direction, up or down.

Next, he had to have a specific instrument to create the hedge against his portfolio, attacking the risk of a down stock market. He decided to buy QQQ puts at the money when his indicator noted a Down market, and sell those same puts, going flat with no option position in an Up market, leaving his aggressive portfolio unhedged.

Since his strategy was now in place, what did he have to do right away? The stock market was currently in an up direction, so he did nothing. No need for hedges when the wind is in your favor. He started reviewing his direction indicator every day and prepared to buy an at-the-money put on QQQ the moment his indicator showed the direction had shifted to down.

Let's look at it from an All-Weather Investing viewpoint. Did Tim realize that risk existed? Yes. Did Tim realize the risk came in the form of a down stock market? Sure. Did Tim decide to exploit that risk using an investing instrument to protect the rest of his portfolio? Absolutely. Tim has created his version of an All-Weather portfolio that will work for him and reduce his exposure to future significant down stock markets.

Let's review another example...

Jennifer is at the end of her career. After successfully riding an extended bull market for years and saving a portion of her above-average salary and bonuses, her portfolio had grown to the size where she could think about retirement. However, her observation was that over her career, she had seen some wild swings in stocks that had resulted in some significant ups and downs in her own portfolio. Thinking about retirement and imagining swings in the value of her portfolio with no career to pay for everyday expenses was a bit daunting. When her portfolio was volatile in the past, she had almost ignored it, because she was so busy having a successful career. However, leaving the working world meant living off her portfolio, something she had no experience doing.

Having an engineering background and knowing a little math, Jen started searching for ways to attack the risk that she believed existed in the stock market. She used a brokerage service with access to global markets and realized that she could manage some of the risk she saw in the markets. If she could simply set up a way to "time" the markets, she could sell stocks that had been very profitable and simply put those proceeds from the sale into a money market fund and earn interest. In Up markets, she would maintain exposure to stocks and the Up market. In Down markets, she would exit her stocks, avoiding at least some of that risk, and ride it out earning interest. Since the largest part of her portfolio would be in her IRA rollover from her large pension plan, there would be no tax consequence of realizing profits on her profitable stocks. She decided that after retirement, she would have the time and interest in managing her stock market risk and creating an All-Weather approach that she could feel comfortable with.

Was her approach All-Weather? Yes. It deals with both Up and Down markets. Was it doable? Yes, she felt she would have the time each day to update her indicators on the stocks she owned. Was it tax efficient inside her IRA? Yes. There would not be taxable consequences of the sale of stocks. It seems to me that Jen has created an All-Weather strategy that targets her concerns on market risk.

How about another...

Ben ran a retail center for farmers and grew his business a great deal over the years. His pension and taxable portfolios were large. Ben's business had a lot of contact with farmers over the years, and they had always talked about hedging their crops. Some of the largest farm operations that he did business with seemed to understand how to remove some of the wild swings in commodity pricing from their own farm operations by using futures contracts to lock in favorable prices in the commodities they used, such as energy or feed, and locking in the price of the commodities they produced, like soybeans, corn, hogs, or cattle.

Ben had a couple of large portfolios to manage and thus far had used a financial advisor to get recommendations on what investments he should own. With his time very precious and having zero interest in trying to manage his portfolio, he asked his advisor about how to get more All-Weather concepts into his portfolio.

After a search through his firm's research platform, Ben's financial advisor found a few funds that incorporated one or more All-Weather Investing concepts outlined in this book. They agreed on one that made sense and bought some of that fund for Ben's portfolios. Was this move All-Weather? Yes. Ben's portfolios were moved over time to more All-Weather choices. Could Ben handle this new All-Weather approach? Sure, since he really had little to do day-to-day in the process, allowing him to run his business.

MONITORING YOUR PROGRESS

We noted technological advancements in the Introduction of this book and how they have sped up and simplified many of the things we do as investors. Mobile apps place real-time info into our pockets and improve the speed at which we can control our investments. These advancements have opened doors to retail investors who have been stuck on the wrong side of bolted entryways for too long.

From pieces of paper, a pencil, and a calculator to personal computers in the '80s, to cell phones and tablets that have more computing power than early mainframe computers, information flows ever more freely. This allows the investor to act or get information to make decisions so much more easily than forty years ago. I have my share of knowledge of computers and the experience to use them wisely, but I had to work to acquire those skills. I had to dig it out of the data and experience the potential emotional roller coaster ride before learning how I could tolerate and smooth out that ride.

I have spent many years developing each of my individual All-Weather Investing strategies and all that hard work up front has paid off. I feel like I have sound structures in place and understand what I have to do each day to update my indicators, adjust my position sizes if necessary, and move on to other activities in my life. I know that with aspects of extreme diversification, hedging, timing, and sideways strategies, I can manage at least some of the risks that I know exist in the markets.

You, too, can spend some time simulating various approaches to All-Weather Investing to find your best fit. Excel spreadsheets are very powerful these days. A simple laptop costs very little and can perform some seriously large calculations. Doing your own homework will increase the confidence in your complete strategy. That confidence will show in your ability to produce positive results.

Perhaps you don't know where to start. If you want some simple examples on trading indicators and position sizing, my website enjoytheride.world has an ETR Trading Tool for Excel that includes some simple things you can do to get started. Check out some of the items on the Learn Store.

For those looking for other ways to crunch data, you might want to look at more robust computer software. The world keeps creating faster and more powerful ways of analyzing data. There are inexpensive courses in programming held online. I've taken some recently at Udemy.com for only fifteen dollars. Go at your own pace. Create some simple programs and work your way up the learning curve.

It doesn't have to be complex. You don't need to train like an Olympic athlete to know how to operate a spreadsheet or create a simple program to run your indicators and position-sizing algorithms.

But you need to get started.

13

MAXIMIZE YOUR RETURN-TO-RISK RATIO

NO MATTER WHAT YOU DEVELOP FOR YOUR OWN personal All-Weather strategy, you will want to maximize your return-to-risk ratio. The problem you will face trying to do this is that many indicators that are commonly used to calculate return-to-risk have flaws or don't apply to your individual portfolio. I will briefly run through some of the popular ones, then offer a better solution.

SHARPE RATIO

This is one of the most widely used ratios for typical stock portfolios and institutional investments. This ratio uses the annualized return over time divided by the standard deviations of those returns over time. It presumes that volatility equals risk and that volatility to the downside is equal to volatility to the upside. This is ridiculous; no client I have ever managed money for ever complained to me about the upside deviations in their account!

MAR RATIO

This ratio divides the annual compounded growth rate (ACGR) over time by the maximum drawdown over that same history. I completely understand that drawdowns are where investors get nervous, so that makes some sense. However, this ratio uses the SINGLE MAXIMUM DRAWDOWN. It doesn't include all the other smaller drawdowns, even those that lasted for a long time. The longer a drawdown lasts, the more likely investors will lose patience or become frustrated by the strategy.

RETURN TO AVERAGE DRAWDOWN

This ratio corrects the flaw of the MAR Ratio. The Return to Average Drawdown takes the ACGR over a period and divides it by the average of ALL the drawdowns that occurred over the period measured. This might be useful, but it doesn't consider the impact that a severe maximum drawdown could have on investor psychology. During a maximum drawdown the investor will be stressed to the maximum.

TREYNOR RATIO

This ratio is similar to the Sharpe Ratio but uses movement of the portfolio relative to a suitable index (Beta), rather than the standard deviation of the portfolio. If you select various benchmarks, you will get a different Beta of the portfolio, and therefore calculate a different Treynor Ratio. I don't like the dependence on human selection of a benchmark index to then affect the Beta and play games with the Treynor Ratio. It lends itself to manipulation.

SORTINO RATIO

This is my favorite of the return-to-risk measurements often included on research platforms. This ratio starts with the same concept as the Sharpe Ratio, which uses standard deviation of returns as the definition for risk. It then changes the calculation and takes only the standard deviation of the *downside* returns the portfolio has seen over the period. This is getting closer to what investors and traders would view as risk but doesn't consider time spent in those risk periods.

A MORE MEANINGFUL RETURN-TO-RISK RATIO—THE ETR COMFORT RATIO

Working for clients and managing my own money have taught me a lot about how the equity curve going up or down can cause the human element to modify or mess up the investing process.

It always amazes me to see those flashy track records out there with 50 percent drawdowns that show excellent long-term compound average growth rate (CAGR) performances that are sold to investors. There is no way that any typical human being on the planet will stick around for that long-term record when they see their portfolio down 50 percent. Most can't even last through more than a 15 to 20 percent down period!

Then what causes clients and traders to pull the plug on a strategy due to performance? I would propose two different things: depth of a drawdown past where they are comfortable and the time spent in those down periods. In other words, very few investors would be rattled with a 5 percent down period, but after a few years it would wear thin. On the other hand, a quick 30 percent down period might also cause many to abandon their plans immediately.

The way I see it, traders and their clients need comfort to keep doing what they are supposed to be doing. As soon as they get past their discomfort threshold, they move on to the next great idea.

Having an engineering degree lends me different perspective on the calculation of return-to-risk. I decided to use concepts from integral calculus to create a simple measure of the amount of discomfort caused by the magnitude of the down period *and* the time spent in that period of discomfort. On the positive side of things, periods of new highs are great, and the trader has comfort. None of my clients complained about making new equity highs. I developed that into:

ETR Comfort Ratio = Amount of Comfort/Amount of Discomfort

Next, we need to include a few parameters that capture how much of a down return causes discomfort (**Drawdown Return Threshold**) and how long a drawdown lasts before the trader would experience discomfort (**Drawdown Time Threshold**). For most investors, something like at least 10 percent down or six months in a drawdown would make you think about changing what you are doing.

The Amount of Discomfort would be the sum of the magnitude of the current drawdown during each period spent in that drawdown over the selected drawdown thresholds. As soon as the thresholds are exceeded, you would start summing each period's current drawdown value until the portfolio gets back to new highs and you return to comfort levels.

The Amount of Comfort would be the reverse of the Amount of Discomfort. Whenever you get to new highs and move up from there, you would keep track of that surge up. The surge is the percentage the current upswing climbs above the end of the last drawdown. You would sum every period's current surge until the next drawdown threshold is exceeded. At that point you would be back to summing the period's current drawdown to the Amount of Discomfort. The Amount of Comfort would essentially be the time and magnitude spent in periods of comfort. The more profits the portfolio enjoys, and the more time spent in surges, the larger the Amount of Comfort.

The ETR Comfort Ratio would then be a simple ratio of the Amount of Comfort to the Amount of Discomfort.

A Simple Example: T-Bills

T-Bills are used in calculations all over the financial universe as "Risk-Free Rate." If the amount of time spent in a drawdown with a T-Bill with very short duration is near or at zero, then almost every day would be a comfort day, making a new high. Almost no days would be spent in down days, so the sum of those days would be near zero.

ETR Comfort Ratio (of T-Bills) = A positive increasing number / 0 = infinity

In other words, T-Bills have a very high ETR Comfort Ratio.

Another Example Using the S&P 500 Index

In a study that I ran a couple of years ago, I pulled the S&P 500 Index monthly values going back to 1993, over twenty years of data. I then created a simple spreadsheet to calculate the monthly ETR Comfort Ratio of the S&P 500 Index and a timed strategy of the S&P 500 Index over time.

GRAPHIC 38—TIMED S&P 500 VS. BUY AND HOLD VALUE OF $1,000 INVESTED (VAMI)

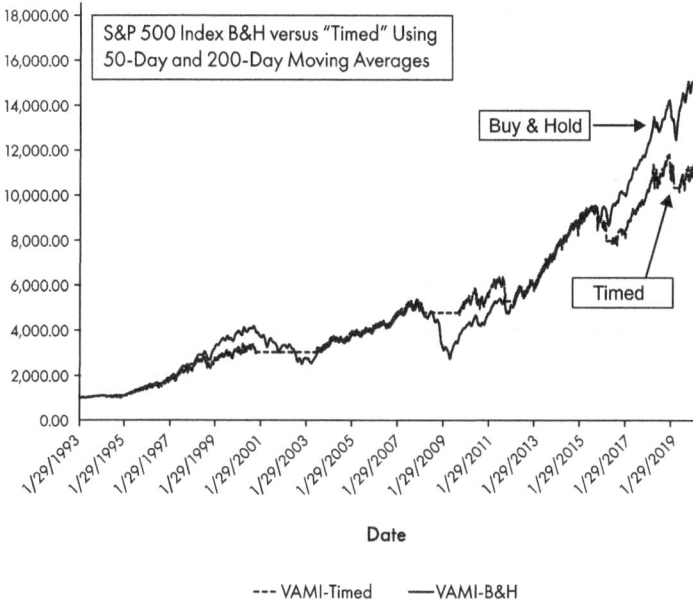

S&P 500 Index B&H versus "Timed" Using 50-Day and 200-Day Moving Averages

Buy & Hold

Timed

Date

--- VAMI-Timed   —VAMI-B&H

GRAPHIC 39—TIMED S&P 500 VS. BUY AND HOLD—ETR COMFORT RATIOS

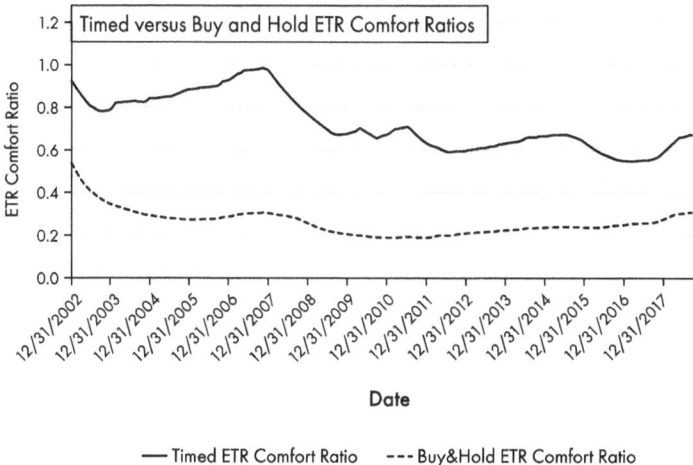

Timed versus Buy and Hold ETR Comfort Ratios

ETR Comfort Ratio

Date

— Timed ETR Comfort Ratio   --- Buy&Hold ETR Comfort Ratio

In Graphic 39 you can see that after you initialize the ETR Comfort Ratio back from 1993 through 2002, the index stays between 0.2 and 0.6 through the end of the data in 2019. The ratio has to have some Comfort periods and some Discomfort periods to create a reasonable calculation. If you used just a Comfort period, you would have the T-Bill situation and an ETR Comfort Ratio of infinity. If you just measured a Discomfort period, you would have zero as your ratio and basically would be saying that you were uncomfortable with the investment over the entire period measured. The period between 1993 and 2022 was used to initialize the ETR Comfort Ratio.

The higher the ratio, the more comfortable you are with the investment. The 2008 bear market really moved the index to extreme lows for the buy and hold approach. However, the timed approach suffered its worst low in 2017. From 2016 on, the comfort ratios of both the timed approach and the buy and hold have steadily moved higher with the recent bull market.

The important thing to note is that the comfort ratio of the timed approach is far above the buy and hold over time. It's not surprising that investors feel more comfortable over the long run in a timed approach to investing than with the conventional "buy and pray" strategy that suffers occasional 50 percent drawdowns. Including timed approaches in your All-Weather strategy will help to increase your ETR Comfort Ratio levels.

AVOIDING THE COMMON MISTAKES

MARKETS ARE APATHETIC TOWARD INVESTORS. THEY wouldn't care if a single loss wiped out your entire portfolio. Nor would they care if your assets varied so widely that an entire economic crash wouldn't make a dent in your portfolio. Bear markets and bull markets will continue to exist in a seesaw battle between buyers and sellers, regardless of anything you might do with your trading.

Of course, no investor would mind being caught with long stocks in an extensive bull market. But a bull market won't last forever. Rough times are bound to hit every market, and it's important to protect yourself from unexpected drawdowns.

In so many aspects of life, people are quick to call it quits after a bit of turbulence. Yet in these moments we can learn and improve upon what we do. These rough patches and bad reactive decisions can be used as your motivators to continue learning and to gradually make fewer mistakes.

Many individual investors, especially those new to investing, exit trading the markets altogether based on a few wrong decisions. If there isn't a support group of like-minded people around you, it can be hard to overcome these mistakes. However, a simple mindset adjustment can be the cure.

Think of mistakes like a bad tee shot in golf. You are aiming for the fairway, but you slice the ball, and it heads into the rough. What do you do? You want to slam the heel of your club into the soft, green grass, right? But you don't. You mutter a few words under your breath, walk back to your bag, and analyze what you could have done better.

The best part? There's still a way out. Even if a tree trunk the size of your golf cart sits between your ball and the flag, there's still a way to punch the ball out into the fairway and play from there. It might not be the ideal situation, but there's still something to be done.

You wouldn't quit and leave your ball in the rough, would you? Would you leave your cart on the path with your clubs still strapped to the back and walk home after a bad shot? No way. You'd try to pick up the pieces and promise yourself that the next hole will be better. The same should go for your investments.

You'll make mistakes while trading. That's inevitable especially at a time when prices and markets are moving at much higher speeds than ever before. When everything moved slower in the '70s and '80s, it wasn't as common to see people jump into investing without doing some research. It wasn't even possible to do so. Back then, you needed to pick up the phone, call your financial advisor or broker, ask for current prices, wait for the return phone call, then decide your next move. You might take an entire day to initiate a new investment. You had time to think through your decisions.

Today you need only press your finger on the screen of your phone, and you've made a trade. For the inexperienced trader, this could lead to trouble.

NOT HAVING A COMPLETE STRATEGY

Periodically someone will message me on a social media platform with something like, "I bought XYZ stock at $X and it now is up to $Y. What should I do with it?" That most certainly is not a trading strategy. If all the boxes we mentioned back in Chapter 4 are not addressed, you have an incomplete strategy. This means that you haven't thought through what you will do in Up, Down, and Sideways markets. You have not figured out your position-sizing rules. You have no contingency plan for unexpected events. Perhaps you have not done a great job of figuring out how you intend to execute this strategy perfectly. Any one of these things can throw your plan out of whack. Create a complete strategy and execute it flawlessly, and you'll have a lot less stress when strange events visit you. As a reminder, I reproduced my view of a complete trading strategy in Graphic 9.

GRAPHIC 9—A COMPLETE TRADING STRATEGY

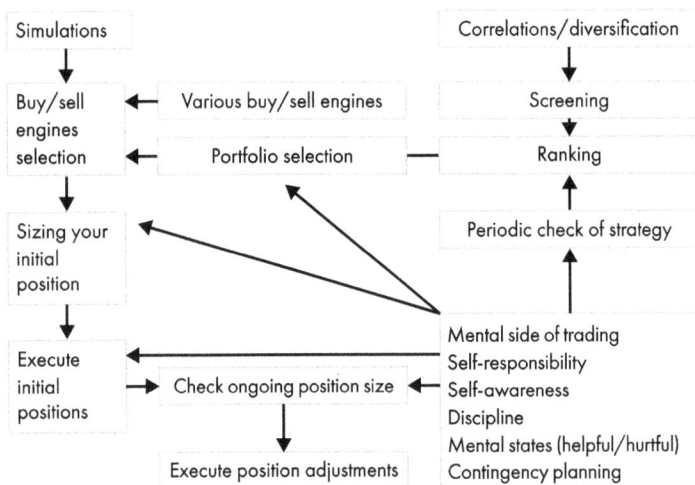

Study each box in this chart and ask yourself, "Have I figured out that aspect of my trading yet?" If not, give it some thought and come up with a plan. Those traders I run into that are struggling will typically be missing something in Graphic 40.

NOT PROPERLY SIZING YOUR POSITIONS

Since I spent an entire chapter of this book and wrote a whole book on properly sizing your positions, I'll spare you the repetition. This chapter is on avoiding common mistakes. One common mistake I see traders making is not having a consistent and logical method of sizing and managing their position size on each investment.

The "I think this stock is really going to move, I'll pick up more of it" method of sizing your position is not a path to trading success. Yes, you may be correct on that trade, and you find yourself with a big winner. But over the next 1,000 trades, if you keep trading that way, you will find some trades along the way that will kick you in the teeth. They will do severe damage to the portfolio.

The other side of the situation is also true. You do your homework on a stock, and you are about to buy a properly sized 1,000 shares. But that little voice says, "The market looks a little toppy right now, and I'm not sure that this company will do well if inflation fires up." You end up talking yourself into buying only 500 shares and it becomes your best investment of the year. Your portfolio doesn't get the full benefit of the position because you decided to buy half your "normal" size on this one. You then proceed to berate yourself for not following your simple trading strategy because you "knew better." I've done it, and it's not beneficial to your trading psyche.

You should have a consistent method to size your positions. If you don't, head back to Chapter 10: How Much Do We Buy or Sell? Avoiding this common mistake is simple. "Just do it!" as Nike's famous slogan said.

FAILING TO DIVERSIFY

Investors often overlook diversifying into additional markets because it takes more time and energy to research, create strategies for, and execute trades in additional markets. At the time of writing this book, I own some fifty-plus positions across twenty exchange traded funds, thirty-one futures markets, and stock index option spread across nine different strategies. It takes me between forty to eighty minutes each day to update all my orders for the next twenty-four hours. Admittedly, I've had many years of practice in trading, so I'm going to have an advantage there, but someone who has mastered the routine of managing a stock portfolio could take a look at some of the micro futures contracts and create a separate strategy for those. Maybe look at a weekly approach for selling some index option spreads.

I'm not saying that you need to jump into fifty markets with dozens of strategies overnight. You would likely need to bring some computer power, and that would take a great deal of time. However, every trader out there could consider diversifying more. I'm not talking about adding one more growth stock to your growth stock portfolio. That's not going to provide much All-Weather effect if the general stock market heads into a -50 percent bear market.

Maybe select a precious metals sector ETF? Maybe choose a hedging strategy timed with indicators to go on only during down moves? Maybe pick five extremely diversified micro futures contracts that have nothing whatsoever to do with the stock market, and trade them with a simple indicator and position-sizing algorithm to ramp up your experience? Do not get stuck in a rut with your portfolio. Trading is trading. Now that I have done it for nearly fifty years, I find trading futures easier in many ways than trading individual stocks.

One simple example of this is using ETFs in different sectors of the economy. ETFs are simple to invest in because they are exchange traded and can diversify you across a number of stocks with one trade. When you go even further and diversify your ETFs by spreading your money across ETFs in non-correlated markets, you achieve some diversification. One sector's collapse may hurt you a little, but you're not out of the game.

Go back to Chapter 7: Extreme Diversification for ideas on spreading your risks.

Avoid the mistake of not diversifying by examining what you now trade and asking the simple question, *"What else is out there that I could use to diversify the portfolio and make it more All-Weather?"*

CONFUSING A BULL MARKET FOR BRAINS

As you continue to monitor and adjust your strategy, remember that bull markets can be dangerous because some people confuse them with talent. Don't confuse a bull market with brains. Keep an eye on the trends and keep your emotions and ego out of it.

Over the past fourteen years dating back to the time following the 2008–2009 economic crash, the stock market has performed pretty well. The COVID pandemic barely had an effect on stocks, seeing a drop of about 35 percent over a short span before heading to all-time highs again. Since then through the end of 2021, things have been moving uphill so quickly it's tough to keep up. Everybody active in equities at the end of 2021 could claim that they were making profits and doing the right thing in their trading.

But then came the 2022 bear market. The TV pundits quickly went from predicting how high the stock market will go to predicting where the bottom of the bear market is going to be.

It's great to be making gains in your portfolio, but remember that a complete reversal is only one government regulation or world news event away. It is important to realize that nothing is guaranteed. *The market will do what the market will do.* Knowing this allows you to properly attack the risk in your profile rather than foolishly ignoring risk and allowing it to visit you.

STARTING WITH TOO LITTLE CAPITAL

I talk to traders around the world, some with very little to trade and others with millions. I can say without any doubt that large portfolios have an easier time adapting an All-Weather strategy to their investments. Small portfolios will have higher costs as a percent of equity and less ability to diversify by instrument, strategy, market, or time period. This will always lead to smaller portfolios having more granular, erratic, and less predictable returns, along with increased risks.

Often, a trader is in a job he doesn't love and gets so into trading that he wants to go full time but doesn't have enough capital to pull that off. He asks, "What advice can you give me on becoming a full-time trader?" I suggest staying in his current situation and dumping as much extra money into his trading account as he can. *So many aspects of what I am talking about in this book are made easier with a larger portfolio. Make it a priority.*

NOT COMPLETELY UNDERSTANDING WHAT YOU ARE DOING

Many times when traders see a great idea involving some new option or instrument, they are ready to jump on board. They don't really understand how these new things work, but off they go using them. That can lead to disaster when you encounter risk, and the new instruments end up doing damage. I like to first read a lot about and test any new potential investment strategy, then start with an extremely small position in the new idea. If my understanding of what happens meets my expectations, I can then ramp up the investment or strategy to full size. *Research new instruments like futures or options before using them to diversify.*

NOT CONSIDERING COSTS

Any trading strategy will have various costs of implementation. Commissions are one of the first that come to mind, but some brokers in the stock arena have taken those to zero dollars. There still is a bid/ask spread on every investment, and that costs you money over time. Liquidity in an investment will tend to minimize the bid/ask spread costs, so you might screen for possible investments that have high liquidity.

When you buy and sell in a normal taxable account, you are likely to have tax consequences with your profits and losses. *Make sure that if you have had some profitable trades, you earmark some of the portfolio for complying with your tax obligations.*

COMPARING YOUR PORTFOLIO TO OTHERS' PORTFOLIOS

Implementing and executing your strategy depends on you. The markets in which you invest and the strategies you use depend upon your own life situation. It's important to remember that those life situations that differentiate you from your fellow investors will also contribute to the way your strategic plan operates.

Run your own plan that works well with your own profile. Know your risk tolerance levels and invest with those in mind. Don't look at those around you and wonder what they're doing. If your neighbor says he just had a great quarter in the market, don't inquire about his strategy and try to mimic it. Why? One, because markets change quickly. And two, because his strategy will likely not suit you and your situation.

The same is true if that same neighbor has a tough stretch of time while your portfolio reaches all-time highs. If you find success and trading longevity with an All-Weather Trading approach, I would be more than happy to hear that you shared this book or this philosophy with them. However, in the short term, keep your head down, remain focused on your portfolio, and don't worry about what others are doing.

Social media has thousands of traders talking about all sorts of positions they are buying, strategies that they are making a killing with, and predictions of what is going to happen next week with XYZ. What does this have to do with your well-constructed, well-thought-out plan? Absolutely nothing! *Execute your plan flawlessly! Avoid distracting yourself with information that should not play any part in your plan.*

NOT CONSIDERING YOUR SCHEDULE AND COMMITMENT

Your schedule is something that should be factored in. How much time will you have to develop a complete All-Weather strategy? How much time can you allot each day or week to execute your strategy? Do you have a family who needs your attention, or is your nest empty? Do you have a full-time occupation that has limited flexibility? Do you travel a lot with a constantly changing schedule of events?

Certain strategies will take more time or need to be monitored more often. If work takes you out of the country for two weeks or if you need to be available at the drop of a hat to pick up a sick child from school, you will want to stay away from certain trading strategies. You don't want to set up techniques that are going to intrude on your personal life and important obligations.

The less time you have, the more long-term and hands-off you need to be. The more details you want to get involved in and the more time and desire you have, the more likely you'll want to concentrate on shorter-term investment strategies. The more experienced you are, the more able you are to handle increased volatility. The less experienced you are, the more you should favor a less volatile path. The correct answer will be different for each All-Weather Trader. Customizing what you do for you is the best road to success.

Those looking for a lot of action with time to spare and a reliable day may even want to consider day trading. Risks per trade can be small, returns can be compounded, and it doesn't require millions in capital. I would say that few people I run into would fit this blueprint and are cut out for the life of a day trader with the focus required to perform well.

More traders I run into have limited time, day jobs, family obligations, and limited knowledge about what they are doing. Your living situation, marital status, short-term plans, long-term plans, and plenty of other variables come into play. Those who fail to consider these important factors usually end up making costly mistakes and become frustrated.

Take an honest look at your life and what commitments you can make to trading. Believe me. The markets don't care if your personal life is full of crisis or personal obligations. They will still open and close at the same time each trading day like the sun rising and setting. The markets won't know if you're having a rough day or a good day. Plan a strategy that you can execute with what you believe will be your typical day/week. *Do not try to trade in a way that you know you will not be able to consistently execute.*

INCONSISTENCY

Set it and forget it. This is an expression that has found its way into the investment industry. Think of busy professionals like doctors, lawyers, and business leaders. They have little time outside of their occupation to pay attention to the ongoing changes in the markets. For this reason, they seek professional assistance and pay a small fee in exchange. They are aware of their inability to focus enough attention on the markets to have positive results in their portfolios. Due to their busy schedules, they know that they won't be able to remain consistent with their time. Therefore, they hire someone else to make sure that a strategy is applied to their portfolios over time.

Keeping up with a trading strategy will take some consistent work. It doesn't take a demanding occupation to lose focus and become inconsistent. Anyone can fall into this. You need to remain consistent in your hands-on approach, and good things will come. But that's true in many areas of your life.

Exercise, for instance, is something you should consider. Finding time to do twenty or thirty minutes of cardio three times per week can do wonders for your overall health. At first, you may be sore and tired. But over time, as you remain consistent with it, your body will be healthier, and you will reap the rewards of your continued efforts. If you start to slip up and skip workouts, however, you could slide back to where you started and find yourself frustrated.

The same is true with managing a trading strategy. It doesn't have to take all day. Even if I'm on vacation on a cruise ship in the South China Sea (although I did this once and I don't recommend it), I can find my typical forty to eighty minutes somewhere between the markets' closing today and opening tomorrow. I pull down the data, process some strategies that are more automated, and move stops on some that aren't as automated. When the process is done, I'm good for twenty-four hours until I have to do it again. It's like the exercise example. When you do it every day, you get faster at it, and you find ways to make the process more efficient. Perhaps a little computer automation here and/or a spreadsheet can help you with speeding up your market updates.

Avoid inconsistency. It will make your trading more chaotic and less reliable. Inconsistency will increase the odds of your becoming frustrated with your trading. *If you design things in the first place to strive for consistency, you'll be ahead of a lot of other traders.*

LACK OF MENTAL REHEARSAL

Although being an All-Weather Trader requires attacking risk and attempting to avoid significant losses, common mistakes can still lead to undesirable results. All-Weather Investing is about putting processes in place. It's about strategizing, researching, diversifying, and executing. Those Buy-Sell Engines introduced in Chapter 4? They are tools that shouldn't be shoved into a drawer and forgotten about. They should be present and used consistently for their original purpose.

When those indicators turn green and tell you to buy, do so. When they turn red and tell you to get out of your position, act, if you haven't already put in a stop order. Don't overthink it. Your emotions are going to be tugging at you and trying to convince you to forget about those indicators you put into place. But doing so would defeat the purpose of all your work on selecting your own Buy/Sell engine.

What about those position-sizing concepts discussed earlier? They exist to help you. Use them. Think through every scenario that you might face in the markets and mentally rehearse executing your plan flawlessly. Imagine yourself being a master trader, smoothly and unemotionally making your moves, calculating your position sizes, and transmitting your orders. No rush, no excitement, and no mistakes.

Remember, one of the benefits of an All-Weather approach is the reduction in stress levels.

When your predetermined strategy is telling you to do something, it's time to make a move. *Use that spreadsheet or trading platform, rehearse what you will do when you are facing various situations, and make the moves you have rehearsed.*

LACK OF CONTINGENCY PLANNING

Life has a way of throwing events at you that can divert or distract you from your plans. You are having a quiet day trading smoothly, and the internet goes down. Or you lose electricity. Or your broker platform is not letting you sign in. Or your broker triples margin requirements for a market that is going crazy due to world events. This stuff happens all the time, yet many traders do not give it a thought when planning out what they will do in trading.

Create some contingency plans. Have backups. Up in the mountains, where I spend my summers in Arizona to get out of the heat, we lost internet service due to a backhoe accidently severing a fiber optic line. My internet backup plan is three-fold. First, I happened to know that a grocery store with a national presence had to have a dedicated internet service for their financially sensitive cashier operations and inventory systems. They are not on the normal local publicly available internet. They have a café where you can eat lunch or grab a coffee. If I didn't get my internet back, I planned on going there and running my trading processes on my laptop through their internet system.

The second backup was a hotspot on my phone. When I travel, I sometimes will find either no internet or such bad internet that it's frustrating to use. If I find I don't have internet, but have phone service, I set up the hotspot and tie into the internet over my phone and run my processes on the laptop. In this particular case, this option was not available to me since the backhoe incident shut down phone service as well!

The third backup for my mountain is to head ninety minutes away to my Scottsdale location. I have great internet service there, and that location would not have been affected by the backhoe incident.

So, was it inconvenient to think of all this ahead of time and plan for it? Definitely. But that day I wasn't stressed out because I had a contingency plan in place and was prepared to put it into action. It turns urns out the fiber optic line was repaired in twelve hours, and I was able to get my work done the normal way, although a little later than normal.

The point is don't wait for life's twists and turns to come your way without having a plan. You can dream up scenarios that will interrupt your normal routine. *Think through what you will do if those things happen, and mentally rehearse executing the contingency plan. It will be a lot less stressful when you really have to run on your alternate plan.*

DON'T LET LIFE GET IN THE WAY

There's another factor to think about when it comes to time commitment, and that's to make sure life doesn't prevent you from getting started in the first place. Are there people in your life who are always talking about things they should have done? Or that they want to start doing but just haven't gotten around to?

Get started. There's never going to be a perfect time to begin some new journey. The best thing to do is to execute. Start studying. Figure out which markets interest you most and the ones that won't be burdensome for your focus. Procrastinating only adds to that psychological pressure that can come with owning or not owning investments. It's simply another of those stressors that you might have to deal with.

Don't let the typical business of life get in the way. Start with an inventory of where you are right this moment. Start figuring out the pieces of a successful trading strategy you already have and the ones you need to obtain. Figure out how much capital you have and how you might push more to your trading account over time. *Think through how much time you have to create and execute a strategy. Start the process today.*

15

ALL-WEATHER INVESTING AND THE FUTURE

INVESTORS ARE ALWAYS LOOKING FOR THE NEXT BIG trend. Professional or amateur, it doesn't matter. Everyone remains on the lookout for the *single* strategy they believe helps them maximize gains with as little risk as possible.

Investing is all about emotion. It's this emotion that takes over and also the fear of missing out (FOMO) on the new, better trend and the profits that might come with it. So many investors place their money in a secure position only to give in to the temptation of something else that is new and shiny. Take cryptocurrencies at the start of 2020 as an example. Prior to 2020, it seemed as if Bitcoin were the only cryptocurrency being used as an investment tool, mostly as a commodity like gold to hedge against inflation.

Since then, new coins and tokens have hit the market at record rates and with soaring prices. But there have also been plenty of cryptocurrencies that have come to the surface and flopped. After all, thousands of currencies in the same market cannot all see increased value. More importantly, volatility has caused some crypto investors to become millionaires while others have lost everything in a very short window of time.

Becoming an All-Weather Trader means designing a more stable, long-term way to deal with investing. Stick with your plan and avoid some of the fad investments that seem to be pushed on investors today. That's not to say investing in cryptocurrencies is bad, because there are gains to be made. I have had a great time trading crypto micro futures over the last two years. However, *allocating too much of your portfolio* or thinking you'll *make a lot of money without any risk* is a mistake.

It's important to look deeper into new, future investing opportunities, but that doesn't mean the typical staples of the investment world are safer either. Look at bond yields in 2022 and the returns made in the bond market. With the FED increasing rates to fight inflation, bonds have not even come close to matching inflation. Investors who are told bonds are a safe bet and pour their funds into that avenue are actually losing net wealth over time. Then bonds, typically thought of as a safe investment, aren't really without risk.

Stocks are dealing with the same issue. They are overvalued and becoming increasingly more volatile. Retail investors chasing tech stocks could see gains in the short term, but the long-term potential includes a great deal of unknown and unprotected risk.

Most investors do not know what they will do should we have yet another down 50 percent market as we have had numerous times in history. Buy and hold will be a frustrating ride.

There's never been a riskier time to be an investor. Bull and bear markets cannot last forever. If you think that stocks will continue to rise 5 to 10 percent every year for the rest of time, go buy an index fund and enjoy the steady ride. But risk works both ways. As an All-Weather Trader, you'll be attacking negative risk and trying your best to keep it managed. At the same time, you'll be thinking about ways to take that risk and turn it into a positive for your portfolio.

Remember the goal: less negative risk and more positive risk.

There are chaotic events all the time. One government action or news item is all it takes to send the markets moving in a direction that hurts your portfolio. It's your job to make sure your portfolio is protected from such events.

DETERMINING RISK FOR THE FUTURE

The future will include chaotic moments. It's inevitable. These are what people are trying to avoid. However, wishing there wasn't as much chaos will not make it disappear. If anything, it seems to me that chaotic market moves have been occurring even more frequently as time marches on.

It's important to know that risk means different things to different people. The first is short-term risk of volatility. This is the risk people usually think of first; they worry about how much they will lose in the short term if markets move a certain direction. This is important to deal with on a day-to-day basis, but what about some long-term risks?

What if bonds lose for ten years as they did in the '70s and early '80s?

What if stocks go down 90 percent as they did during the Great Depression?

What if stocks go down 60 percent as they did in 2008, but they don't come back up (like they did in 2009)?

What if nothing in the 60 bonds/40 stocks strategy (that favorite of financial advisors) works?

The people concerned with some of these longer-term risks aren't concerned with short-term volatility. They think about longevity over short-term results, both good and bad. After all, why does the All-Weather Trader invest? We eat risk and volatility that others aren't willing to go near and, in return, we make gains in our portfolio.

Consider this when you begin looking into the future of your portfolio. Avoiding risk doesn't mean avoiding the daily, weekly, or quarterly ups and downs that occur in a normal market. That is essentially worrying about random noise that won't knock you out of the game. You're looking to avoid the risk to your long-term plan.

By creating an All-Weather approach, the risks that come with inevitable changes and movements in the future are somewhat hedged. By creating an overall strategy that you can live with for a very long time, you can survive through all sorts of chaos. You can watch the world panic around you and feel secure knowing you have a plan. You've mentally prepared for the chaos and how you will react to it, continuing to execute your plan perfectly.

In the spring of 2020, during the first parts of the COVID panic's down move in stocks and extremely huge moves in many other markets, many Commodity Trading Advisors simply stopped trading. They felt these moves were insane, and stocks looked like they were melting down fast. Treasuries were a favorite safe haven for many. The stock market declined rapidly by over 30 percent.

I stayed with my strategies. I was hedged on my stock exposure. I was killing it in palladium futures contracts and short energy contracts, which ultimately ended up going to negative prices. These were huge moves that only come along once in a very long while. And I was in on all of them watching my portfolio's equity screaming upward. When appropriate, I peeled off partial positions to manage my exposure, so even with record-breaking volatility, I maintained my composure every day.

Next came the cries on social media: "Is this the bottom?" and "It isn't time to buy yet. Wait for the test of the lows." Only there was a problem with these predictions: a test of the lows never happened this time around. The market will do what the market will do. Traders who fearfully fled the markets during the downswing were now agonizing over missing the move up that was happening fast. I ran my unchanged All-Weather processes every day through this record volatility. The stock hedge came off; I had lots of new buy signals on my long sector ETFs, and I became fairly fully invested long in stocks while reversing many of my futures positions.

The result? I had the most profitable year of trading in my life with returns over 100 percent. I'm not telling you this story to brag since I didn't do anything special or anything different from what I do in boring fashion every day. I didn't predict the chaos that COVID would bring the world. I didn't predict how long the jabs would take to develop or how the markets would react to all the news.

What you can learn from my example is that if you've thought through and have plans for chaotic times, you can remain calm and carry on. The reason that I had such a profitable year was opportunity meeting action. I had nothing whatsoever to do with crude oil going to negative prices in 2020. I measured the direction, executed a sell stop order, went short, managed my sizes well, and eventually bought the remaining contracts back and went long. Crude oil is now over one hundred dollars per barrel due to Eastern European tensions. I did not predict a single part of that. I simply managed the process, let the results happen, and enjoyed the ride.

PREDICTING THE FUTURE

Why choose to be an All-Weather Trader? The benefit of using these strategies is that you have a probability of generating positive returns even if bonds and stocks don't trend positively for an extended period. In a world where these are the two most common investment choices, a scenario where they both trend downward could have lasting negative results on your net wealth.

When it comes to forecasting and predicting the future—well, predictions suck. There was a book that came out after Black Monday that talked about two potential possibilities for the markets: a recession or a depression. What happened? Neither. Instead, the markets went on a bull run for over a decade.

In 1989, Japan was the second-largest economy in the world, primed to take over the U.S. as number one. If in 1989 you would have told *anyone* that Japan would enter a thirty-five-year bear market, you would have been laughed out of the room. But that's exactly what happened.

Nobody can predict the markets; that's why there's so much risk involved. But that risk is what brings the reward. Anybody who claims they can make accurate predictions is trying to sell you something, and it's most likely not going to be something that will last for ten, twenty, or thirty years.

An All-Weather Trader can understand where he will produce profits and where he will have lackluster results. It doesn't matter how the markets react. An All-Weather Trading strategy was better than any other strategy back when I first developed my own portfolio concepts, and that's still true today. No matter what sorts of iterations or trends occur in the markets, being an All-Weather Trader is the only way I can see that consistently sees steady, reasonable returns.

Think about what the future holds. And we're not talking about market predictions here. Think about the markets alone. The ease of entry is becoming greater and greater with each passing day. Computers and mobile technology are having a greater presence. Software applications allow more money to be pushed into markets at speeds those markets aren't used to seeing. Volatile periods will be only greater in both frequency and magnitude.

An All-Weather Trader is ready to deal with the chaos that will come if software continues to have that volatility-increasing effect. The only reason you aren't hearing about this approach more often is that money managers haven't discovered a way to relay to clients the positive aspects of being an All-Weather Trader. Some are too big to deal with the size they must move on trades, and others are too worried about keeping up with the large short-term gains a select few are seeing and trying to chase those returns without attacking the risk associated with that. From my experience I can tell you that boring does not bring in vast quantities of new clients with lots of assets.

Keeping up with other money managers is not my reality. I am retired, happy with my life and lifestyle, and want the stability that being an All-Weather Trader brings me. As humans we need some reassurance that our money is safe. It's why we buy so much insurance. But that insurance needs to be in place before the storm comes. Once the signs of a storm appear on the radar, it's too late. Insurance companies won't allow you to start a policy. You need to do so beforehand.

Create insurance on your own assets by implementing an All-Weather approach. Then, you have a plan to deal with whatever comes your way.

STUDY FAILURE

Failure occurs often in our industry, yet the reasoning goes overlooked. Others assume that failure has occurred due to uneducated decisions or bad luck, but there were certainly strategies put into place before the failure occurred.

Everyone studies success, but wisdom lies in studying failure. What were those people who have "failed" attempting to do? What was their mindset? What did they misinterpret? You can learn a lot that other people won't because they only study success stories.

There is a misconception that timing has everything to do with the success of your portfolio. Or that some other single variable is the only important one. It simply isn't true. Studying some of these failures allows you to see the need for a wider, more global approach.

The Argentine Great Depression in 1998 occurred because of its closed economy.

The Russian financial crisis in 2014–2017 happened because it was so heavily focused on its oil exports that when prices dropped nearly 50 percent, it had nothing to fall back on.

The Japanese collapse in 1989 was due to extreme valuations in stocks and real estate.

What did we learn from each of these failures? One thriving asset class can remain so for only a limited time. Eventually, a correction takes place, and that asset should have been hedged or sold. As an All-Weather Trader, I've got so many different, uncorrelated investments in my portfolio at one time, there's always something that might be moving and helping the portfolio on its path to success. When one market has a rough time, other parts of the strategy can pick up the slack.

TAKE THIS APPROACH AND RUN WITH IT

As I have reiterated, the 60/40 approach is one of the most common methods used by retail investors. It's safe yet allows the potential for growth. With 60 percent of your assets in stocks, you have enough skin in the game to see some growth to match your future goals. And with 40 percent in bonds, you have a typically slower-moving investment to diversify the portfolio and buffer potential stock losses along the way.

Extremely diversified All-Weather Investing is conceptually similar to a 60/40 method with a lot more levels of safety added into the mix. It's nothing incredibly exciting. It's formulaic. It finds the risk in various markets and attacks those risks, attempting to yield rewards.

Our goal here is to be bored with success. Not every win has to be done in a mad dash to the finish line. When was the last time you watched an exciting marathon?

Remember, there are only four steps you need to properly get started with this strategy:

1. Choose markets that fit your personality and goals.

2. Implement a Buy/Sell engine that tells you when to buy and when to sell (and act on it).

3. Know your portfolio asset level and how much you will risk to each position, sizing those positions consistently.

4. Have longevity in mind and prepare for the curveballs that markets will throw you.

It seems simple, but many have a hard time with simple. Investors tell me all the time, "Surely if you are going to be successful in investing, it has to be complicated." That's the thinking of so many investors. It is only simple if you have the mental discipline to execute it impeccably. You must abide by the strategies and rules you put in place. Use the readily available software to manage your investments or hire someone else to manage them. Whichever your option, you have plenty of tools to help. It all depends on which you want to exchange: a fraction of your earnings for a hands-off approach with someone else handling the day-to-day actions or time and research for a hands-on approach. Neither is wrong. The only wrong option is attempting to avoid risk by avoiding the markets. With inflation, that decision will likely result in a net loss of wealth over the long run. This is similar to what happened to my dad with the CDs.

Opportunities are out there. Don't get lured into the buy and hold trap. You can author an amazing plan for yourself, creating generational wealth and setting up you and your family for financial wellness while always enjoying the ride.

CONCLUSION

THE ENTIRE INVESTING ECOSYSTEM REVOLVES AROUND you. The stock market, bond market, futures, cryptocurrencies, mutual funds, private equity—all depend on you. You are the one putting your money into these markets. It's no surprise there are so many options out there in which you can invest. Each market wants to entice you with its attractive offerings.

Think of the psychology behind that. Picture yourself standing in the middle of a room with a dollar bill in your hand and hundreds of others standing in a circle around you, all screaming about why they deserve that dollar of yours and how they can make it grow for you. There's a lot of stress involved in making that decision. But there's also a lot of stress and risk involved in every one of the available markets.

I have tried many different trading styles in my days inside and outside the money management industry and being an

All-Weather Trader has suited me better than any others. Want proof? I haven't written a book explaining any other investment or trading process. This is the culmination of decades of trading experience and arriving at a place mentally where I am totally comfortable with suggesting some of these concepts to other traders struggling to find their way. It's my way of giving back to the industry that has given me so much in my lifetime.

The goal of this book is to make life easier for you psychologically. Listening to promises made by all those people standing around you who are begging for that dollar can be detrimental to your mental health and lead to investment decisions driven by emotion. Typically, investors give all their money to one promising investment concept, or they become so paralyzed by analysis and indecision that they don't make any choice at all; they miss out on any potential gains altogether. Even worse, I've had friends on social media who have been scammed into thinking they were answering direct messaging from me and investing in something promising. In fact, someone had completely copied my profile, photos, and posts and scammed them out of some of their money in a crypto hoax. I never sell investments over social media.

As a trader, you are the one putting your money into an investment strategy, and you deserve the returns. You are providing something of value to the industries into which your dollar goes, and that value should be reciprocated. But you don't get something for nothing. You need to attack the risks inherent in various investments, because hiding from it means hiding from the markets, and you receive no return if you don't provide something of value to the ecosystem. This is true in anything. Whether you're trading stocks or widgets, you don't get something for nothing.

Keep your expectations realistic as you become an All-Weather Trader. Know that drawdowns will occur, and don't panic. If you're making 8 to 10 percent returns year over year, whether trading yourself or through a fund, you're doing better than most. Does your job offer an 8 to 10 percent raise every year? I doubt it.

One last thing to remember is to not gloat about your earnings to those who may not be traveling alongside you on the uphill path. A saying that I have on the wall next to where I trade is "Unless you are humble in the face of the market, the market will see to it that you are humbled." This isn't a competition. It's a long-term puzzle we all are trying to solve. We're playing a four-day golf tournament in the middle of a season of tournaments, not just one hole. We are designing a strategy for our next 1,000 trades, not focusing on the one trade we just completed.

That's it from this All-Weather Trader. I've given you everything I have on how I became an All-Weather Trader. I have given you a variety of ideas that you can work with, adjust, and adapt for yourselves. The toolbox is now yours to use. Create a plan, execute that plan flawlessly, and absolutely *enjoy the ride!*

THE END

ABOUT THE AUTHOR

TOM BASSO

THOMAS F. BASSO, currently retired, was CEO of Trendstat Capital Management, Inc., a Registered Investment and Commodity Trading Advisory (CTA) firm. At its peak, Trendstat managed $600 million for clients worldwide from Scottsdale, Arizona. Tom received an undergraduate degree in chemical engineering from Clarkson University. He received a master's in business administration from Southern Illinois University. He has participated as an Arbitrator for the National Association of Securities Dealers and National Futures Association (NFA), and is a past Director on the NFA Board, representing one of the CTA/CPO seats on the board.

In addition, Tom served on the NFA's technology and standards subcommittee for three years. He served on the Board of Directors of the National Association of Active Investment Managers

(NAAIM) and was a director of CreaMiser, Inc., now a division of Dean Foods, which is the leading provider of bulk cream dispensing in the U.S. He was on the Management Committee of Lamp Technologies, a Dallas-based technology company specializing in back office-outsourcing solutions for the futures and hedge fund industry. In 2019, Tom became Chairman of the Board of Standpoint Alternative Asset Management, which manages a fund with a blend of seventy-five global macro-futures markets and global equities. The fund is managed by Eric Crittenden and gives investors exposure to a single-manager, multi-strategy, multimarket, "All-Weather" approach to investing. The firm manages over $500 million and is one of the top performers in its category (https://www.standpointfunds.com).

His engineering, mathematical, and computer background gave Tom the ability to develop a wide range of investment programs to take advantage of opportunities in the financial markets worldwide. He is currently consulting on a new cloud-based trading simulation and order platform targeted to launch in 2022.

He has authored *Panic Proof Investing,* and he was one of the traders featured in *The New Market Wizards,* a book on successful traders written by Jack Schwager. Tom's book, *Successful Traders Size Their Positions—Why and How?,* has been a hit with traders worldwide attempting to manage their position sizes. Michael Covel's book with Tom, *Trend Following Mindset,* has received wide acclaim from traders learning the process of successful trading.

Tom has been retired since 2003 and enjoys a variety of activities including golf, writing, winemaking, cooking, singing in a few choral groups, working out, traveling with his wife Brenda, and helping traders through his retirement website, https://enjoytherideworld.odoo.com. The site offers books, videos, references, research, webinars, seminars, and other helpful resources for traders.

AUTHOR'S TAGS ON SOCIAL MEDIA

Twitter: @basso_tom

Facebook: https://www.facebook.com/enjoytheride.world

LinkedIn: https://www.linkedin.com/in/tom-basso-7786a01a3

Gettr: @basso_tom

Truth Social: @basso_tom

Telegram: @basso_tom

MeWe: mewe.com/i/tombasso

Parler: @enjoytherideworld

Instagram: https://www.instagram.com/masobasso